KT-521-865

STRAUSS

Richard STRAUSS

Alan Jefferson

The Musicians
General Editor: Geoffrey Hindley
M

Patriotism is not enough
(Nurse Edith Cavell)

Musical Patriotism may be too much
(about Richard Strauss)

Other books by *Alan Jefferson*

The Operas of Richard Strauss in
Great Britain 1910–1963 (Putnam)
The Lieder of Strauss (Cassell)
Delius—Master Musicians Series (Dent)

SBN 333 14649 2

First published 1975 by
Macmillan London Limited
London and Basingstoke
Associated companies in New York, Dublin,
Melbourne, Johannesburg and Delhi

Picture research by Susan Bower

Filmset by BAS Printers Limited,
Over Wallop, Hampshire
Printed in Great Britain by Waterlow (Dunstable) Ltd.

Contents

Chapter 1

Beginnings

Richard Strauss who has been called 'the last of the romantic composers' was born in 1864. He produced his first precocious composition at the age of four and for the next 80 years music flowed from his pen in an almost unbroken stream; his last songs were written in 1948. As he said himself, 'I must compose and go on composing, just as a cow must give milk!' Throughout this immense career his music retained traits of the Romanticism of the late nineteenth century. In a sense then he may seem something of an anachronism—although he was already thirty-six by the year 1900 and he was to go on working for over 48 years beyond that date which appears so crucial on the calendar. Musically, of course, it meant—means—very little more than a signpost to the time. Sibelius, another 'delayed' Romantic, went on composing into the late 1920s while the Romantic inspiration lay behind the work of many of the greatest Soviet composers well into the 1940s. If Strauss was anachronistic he was in good company and his formative influence on twentieth-century music cannot be overlooked or denied.

In the first decade of the new century he was undoubtedly the *enfant terrible* of European music. Debussy may have influenced more composers in a subtler way than Strauss did; but Strauss threatened to change the whole course of music, and in his *Salome* and *Elektra* he brought music to the very threshold of atonality, that is to say a state of events where there is no established key, and the music may take what roots the composer chooses to give it. Then there was a dramatic change in Strauss's next composition which set him on an altogether different path. In this book we shall discover how all this came about.

But to begin at the beginning let us look at the background. The Strauss family—no relation whatsoever to the Waltz Kings of Vienna—can be traced back for five generations before Richard's birth to the early part of the eighteenth century. These early forebears were court ushers or 'lictors' in Upper Bavaria near Weiden, steady civil servants who led ordinary, municipal lives. The individuals come into sharper focus in the person of Johann Urban Strauss, born in 1800. He was an idle fellow, totally dependent upon his father for support even when he put a girl in the family way at the age of 21. She was from the local Walter family, a cut above the Strausses. Her name was Maria and her father was the Master Watchman of Parkstein, and as such was responsible for the town's musical activities (the old English word 'waits', 'town musicians' is derived from the Germanic Wächter 'watchmen'). Maria's child was born on 26 February 1822 and baptized Franz Joseph Strauss, but not long afterwards Johann Urban, the father, disappeared altogether and never bothered with Maria or his son again. The burden of caring for the child fell upon Maria's uncle, Johann Georg Walter, also a town musician of Nabburg in Regensburg. Thus, the composer came of a family which had strong ties with music.

His father, Franz Strauss, brought up in this musical atmosphere, soon developed a great talent for the guitar and also for the French horn, a capricious instrument which needs considerable training, aptitude and self-confidence in its player. Franz Strauss also learned to play the violin and the viola, and very soon became self-supporting, unlike his father. In 1845 he applied to the Bavarian government for citizenship, perhaps so that he might start afresh in surroundings untainted by his parenthood, but more likely because of a job which he intended to take. This was as a horn player in the Munich Court Orchestra, but with the introductory task of court guitarist. Strauss rose quickly to become first horn in the orchestra, and played in the premières of

Strauss at the age of twenty-four years in 1888.

Bräu-Bierhallen
Braustübl

Above: Alexander Ritter (1833–1896) was married to Wagner's niece and became one of the earliest disciples of Wagnerism, later gravitating to Liszt's Weimar group. He worked in Stettin, Dresden, Schwerin and Würzburg. He was a violinist in the Meiningen Orchestra under Bülow and Strauss, where he met Strauss for the first time and became his musical guardian and advisor, introduced him to programme music and generally encouraged him. It was mainly due to Ritter's kindness that Strauss wrote and composed his opera Guntram*; but Ritter, who was a Catholic, disagreed on religious grounds with the intent of the work and this somewhat estranged the two men. As well as being a Catholic, Ritter was violently anti-semitic (a fact which was trumped up at Strauss's de-Nazification trial, held against him in 1948).*

Top left: Josephine Pschorr Strauss.
Top right: Franz Strauss.
Centre: As a young man in Weimar
Bottom left: Strauss's birthplace, 2 Altheimer Eck, Munich.
Bottom right: Strauss and his sister Johanna (about 1875).

Wagner's operas *Das Rheingold*, *Die Walküre*, *Die Meistersinger* and *Tristan und Isolde* in Munich, under Hans von Bülow. He was the finest horn player in Germany and when asked about this he used to reply 'I do not prove it, I admit it.'

In 1851, when he was not quite 30, Franz Strauss married Elise Sieff, daughter of an army bandmaster, and they had two children. But in 1854 Munich was afflicted by a violent cholera epidemic in which Strauss's wife and two children perished. Once again Uncle Walter proved to be a tower of strength in comforting the bereaved man; but gradually overcoming his grief by concentrating on his work, Strauss was appointed as a professor to the Munich Academy, and then courted one of the five daughters of a local brewing family. Her name was Josephine Pschorr. At this time in Germany there was a strict social structure (or *Kreis*) so defined as to make it almost impossible for a person from one stratum to marry into another. Although in trade, the Pschorrs were in a higher *Kreis* than a mere musician; but Franz Strauss was, in addition, a professor and a prominent member of the Court Orchestra. So the wedding between Franz Strauss and Josephine Pschorr was allowed to go ahead and took place in Munich on 29 August 1863. Ten months later, on 11 June 1864, Richard Georg was born to them in the Strauss home at 2 Altheimer Eck, behind the Pschorr brewery. This has now been pulled down, but at that time it was in a particularly picturesque and romantic quarter of Munich, which Strauss later called on for the setting of his opera *Feuersnot*.

Franz Strauss was devoted to his son, and apart from the frequent paternal outbursts of rage it was a harmonious family, especially when Richard's sister Johanna was born in 1867. There were times, though, when the almost saintly patience of Josephine Strauss was sorely tried by her husband. On these occasions she would say nothing and would go and sit in the garden and sew, if the weather was fine enough. This was usually a sign that Franz Strauss had been unreasonable. In a way the great Wagner was the cause of these upsets, for nobody irritated and infuriated Franz Strauss more than he did. Wagner was almost afraid of his tongue and used to say 'That fellow Strauss is an unbearable, curmudgeonly fellow, but when he plays his horn one can say nothing, for it is so beautiful.' For his part, Strauss never let a chance go by to rile Wagner and generally contradicted him for the sake of causing a scene. And when Wagner came to write an especially difficult horn part in The Mastersingers he insisted that Hans Richter (later a celebrated Wagner conductor) tried it out first in case Strauss created a fuss. As it was, he told Wagner that he should find out how to write for the horn since what he had given him to play was more suitable for clarinets. Incidents like these left Strauss in a state of high excitement, even when he had gained the point over Wagner; and he brought his bad temper home and let his family suffer with him.

Young Richard grew up in comfortable surroundings and never wanted for anything. They were not a rich family, but Franz Strauss's salary was perfectly adequate especially as they lived first in one Pschorr property and then in another, with the knowledge that there was the substantial brewing fortune behind them all the time. Young Richard started to learn the piano when he was four, with his mother as teacher; and after only six months he was sufficiently advanced to be able to take professional instruction from the virtuoso harpist at the Court Theatre, August Tombo. Six years later he progressed even further, to Carl Niest, the foremost piano teacher in Munich. Strauss was already learning to play the violin as second instrument, and he could scarcely have been in better hands than those of Benno Walter, leader of the Court Orchestra, and his father's first cousin. The way was smoothed for him all the time so that he got the very best tuition from practising musicians, a rare thing for so young a pupil, and usually reserved for master classes. The theoretical side was not neglected either. At the age of eleven, Strauss was placed under the guidance of F. W. Meyer, the Court Conductor, from whom, so he said in later years, he learned everything he needed to know about the whole of musical theory and form, from the basic elements to quadruple fugue. Franz Strauss was always at his side when needed, to advise and suggest, and to guide him in his listening. From an early age the boy was taken regularly to concerts and to performances at the opera so that music was always as much a part of his life as food and drink and parental affection. His experience of music was channelled along the familiar lines of Bach, Haydn and

Beethoven, but especially Mozart. Mozart was Franz Strauss's as well as Richard's musical god. He had everything to give and no one was ever going to be able to come anywhere near him in genius and sublimity. This Richard Strauss always believed, through his father, and upheld Mozart's music as a shining example of excellence.

In the Autumn of 1874, after some coaching at home, Strauss entered the Ludwigsgymnasium, equivalent to a high school, where he remained until 1882. Then he went on to the University with a total exemption in his music matriculation, to study philosophy, but stayed there for only two terms.

His piano and violin playing had become so advanced that at the age of 13, Strauss was allowed to sit at the back desk of the violins in the Wilde Gung'l Orchestra. This was an amateur body of about 30 players which Franz Strauss had formed in 1875 and which he also conducted. Gradually Richard moved up the violin section until he was sitting at the front desk, having absorbed something of orchestral discipline and behaviour. Thereafter he was sometimes allowed to conduct rehearsals of the Wilde Gung'l, particularly if they were working at one of his own compositions.

For Strauss started to compose before he could even write. His first composition of all was a Christmas carol for which he 'painted' the notes, and his mother wrote in the words underneath them. Some of his early works were for school events, such as a production of the 'Electra' of Sophocles, for which he wrote several numbers. All the time he was discarding and re-assessing his new works, which seemed to pour from him with scarcely any effort, so that the early opus numbers can have signified as many as six or seven different compositions until he was satisfied that the most recent one was worthy to remain.

Strauss obtained other, lasting influences from holidays with his family, and from one friend of his school-days. Because Franz Strauss was asthmatic (and eventually had to give up playing the horn for this reason), they all used to travel south to the Alps, to the Black Eagle Hotel in Cortina-Ampezzo. Once there, Strauss used to persuade the landlord to get in a piano for him to play, the priest to let him use the church organ, the school master to talk music with him, and the doctor to accompany him on fishing trips. He must have been a persuasive boy, but from what has come down about him, good company and not in the least priggish.

Strauss's mother had a friend in Innsbruck who was foster-mother to a young man, three years Strauss's senior, called Ludwig Thuille. Thuille was at a music school in Innsbruck, getting a degree, and entered into a corres-

Above: Hans von Bülow (1830–1894). A great supporter of Wagner and the first conductor of Tristan *and* The Mastersingers *in Munich, where he was G.M.D. Afterwards he worked in Hanover, Meiningen (with Strauss as his assistant), Berlin and Hamburg. Strauss learned by example from Bülow's methods and thus was in line with the great conductors of the eighteenth century.*

Below: A view of Munich in 1899. Very little remains of the buildings shown in the picture except for the two celebrated onion domes of the Frauenkirche.

Right: Caricature entitled 'The struggle between the old and the new music' from the magazine Jugend *of 1898. This is possibly the only picture showing Strauss playing the violin. See opposite. While Strauss represents the new music, the other musician symbolizes, with exasperation, the more conservative kind of melody which was then acceptable. (By Reinhold Max Eichler)*

pondence with Strauss that continued between 1877–79. Some of Strauss's letters reveal typically immature impressions, especially of Wagner's operas; but since they are described with such professional knowledge, his adolescent arguments sound a lot more convincing than they really are. At all events, Thuille and Strauss acted as sounding boards for each other, a healthy means whereby they were both able to discuss and exchange their views about 'modern' music: Wagner's and Brahms's. Thuille turned out to be a gifted if conventional musician, a professor of composition at the Munich Academy in 1883 and composer of two operas to libretti which had been intended for Strauss, but which he later gave to his friend.

The most advanced opera to be composed and discussed, though infrequently performed during Strauss's boyhood, was *Tristan und Isolde*. Its score was forbidden in the Strauss household and up to the time when Strauss was 17, he had never heard a note of it. Fortified by curiosity, he one evening took home the piano score and started to play it. The amazing, thrilling music made him oblivious to all else, even the sounds of his father entering the house and going into his room to practise. Suddenly the horn-notes ceased, and Franz Strauss came into Richard's room with his instrument under his arm, unable to believe what he could hear issuing from the piano. He strode up and down in anger, but gradually, as Richard's calm tenor voice answered each of his points rationally and intelligently, the old man stopped criticizing and went back to his own room. *Tristan* was never again discussed. Richard had won his first, decisive battle with his father, and in that moment came of age as an artist and as a man.

Thanks to Wagner's intermittent influence in his life, for good and for not so good, Richard grew in stature. Yet Franz Strauss played at Bayreuth for the first production of *Parsifal* in 1882 and was as rude to Wagner as ever. In the following February, Wagner died, and when the announcement was made to the Munich Court Orchestra, its members all stood in silence as a token of esteem—except Franz Strauss, who remained seated, looking totally unconcerned.

After the death of Wagner, Hans von Bülow, since 1880 the conductor of the Court Orchestra at Meiningen, became one of the great champions of his music despite the fact that years previously his wife Cosima had left him for Wagner. Naturally the older Strauss viewed any admirer of Wagner with distrust but this did not prevent him from calling on von Bülow's assistance in helping to place his son as a conductor. Richard went to see Bülow in Berlin, and not long afterwards he was accepted as his assistant in Meiningen. His professional career had begun.

Below: Ludwig Thuille (1868–1907). Strauss's boyhood friend. Thuille inspired Strauss to listen to and accept 'modern' music but, while they wrote to each other very frequently in the late 1890's, they had drifted apart by the turn of the century

Chapter 2

Strauss the Conductor

Some conductors conduct, others only wag sticks. The difference between them lies in their ability—or otherwise—to project their requirements, personality and interpretation through the musicians under them and upon the work they are playing. It is less important that the players like their conductor, than that his magnetism carries them with him. There are relatively few conductors in any generation whose conducting is a joy to the musicians working for them, and it is a rare thing to find one. But Richard Strauss became one of these. It took some time. The wit and professionalism revealed in his comments on the art go some way to explaining his popularity with orchestras.

Ten Golden Rules for the Album of a young Conductor

1 Remember that you are making music not to amuse yourself but to delight your audience.
2 You should not perspire when conducting: only the audience should get warm.
3 Conduct *Salome*, and *Elektra* as if they were by Mendelssohn.
4 Never look encouragingly at the brass, except with a short glance to give an important cue.
5 But never let the horns and woodwind out of your sight: if you can hear them at all they are still too strong.
6 If you think that the brass is not blowing hard enough, tone it down another shade or two.
7 It is not enough that you yourself should hear every word the soloist sings—you know it off by heart anyway: the audience must be able to follow without effort. If they do not understand the words they will go to sleep.
8 Always accompany a singer in such a way that he can sing without effort.
9 When you think you have reached the limits of *prestissimo*, double the pace. [All this was written in about 1926, but Strauss added in 1948 at this point:] Today I should like to amend this as follows: go twice as slowly (addressed to the conductors of Mozart!)
10 If you follow these rules carefully you will, with your fine gifts and your great accomplishments, always be the darling of your listeners.

His first experience as a conductor came at the very early age of twenty, and then in front of a professional orchestra. He was pitchforked into directing his own Suite for woodwind, Opus 4, by Hans von Bülow, his valued mentor and patron, and conducting it without any rehearsal. Of course Strauss knew the score intimately, but it was not a pleasant occasion for him. He later wrote: 'I do not remember much of what happened since I conducted the whole work in a slight coma'. But it was thanks to this successful effort and to Bülow that he got his first appointment at Meiningen in 1885 where he was paid to learn the repertoire. After only a month, Bülow resigned, leaving Strauss in sole charge of the Court Orchestra.

His next uneasy moment came when the Grand Duchess of Meiningen sailed into the ducal theatre one morning unannounced and demanded to hear the Overture to *The Flying Dutchman*. Great Wagnerian though he was, Strauss had never played this overture and hesitated, then with deference blushed and stood awkwardly. The Duchess suggested tartly that perhaps he could give her the Overture to *Der Freischütz* instead, for *everybody* knew that. Strauss pulled himself together, turned to the orchestra and told them to get out their parts for the *Dutchman* Overture. As he afterwards said, he 'beat time with the courage of desperation', the orchestra helped him through it, and he was saved. Had he not already obtained the sympathy, if not the

Caricature from Jugend *of 1903. 'For his next opera Richard Strauss is preparing a self-contained travelling orchestra!' By A. Schmidhammer.*

A postcard from Meiningen showing the buildings very much as they were in Strauss's time, and with a picture of the theatre which is substantially unaltered

confidence of his orchestra through his ability and consideration for them, it might have been altogether a different story. But Meiningen and its orchestra was too small for Strauss and he was determined to move elsewhere after only six months. In this time he had learned the conventional repertoire, and was able to secure the appointment of third conductor at the Munich Court Opera, in spite of severe warnings from Bülow and from his own father who was still the first horn-player there.

For Munich was, in April 1886 a stronghold of musical reactionaries and while Strauss was welcomed home, with appreciation, it was by no means an ideal appointment. Hermann Levi and Franz Fischer were the first and second conductors, and left Strauss to conduct the works which were considered unfashionable and uninteresting. In addition Strauss had to take the initial rehearsals of most operas for piano run-through; these were unpopular preliminaries and attendance was poor. It offended his tidy and professional mind, and he could not understand how his superiors were able to tolerate such behaviour.

His début in Munich as conductor was *Johann von Paris* by Boildieu, then *Così fan Tutte* and *Maskenball* (*Un Ballo in Maschera*); and from the start his tempi astonished and annoyed his singers. The performance of *Ballo* was given after only one rehearsal, and Strauss had never conducted it before. No wonder then that he wrote to Bülow 'Great carelessness prevails in the matter of rehearsals, which I hope very soon to remedy.' But of course he was unable to make any impression on the set ways of the Munich Opera.

In March 1887 Strauss conducted the première of his *Aus Italien* at a Munich Odeon concert. It was received with booing and catcalls from certain sections of the audience—the expected ones—but Strauss was delighted. Up till this point, Munich's reactionaries had taken it for granted that he was one of them, but now he was proving that he had ideas of his own and meant to enforce them.

Occasional concerts at the Odeon, prestige affairs, were one of Strauss's sidelines there, together with the direction of a women's choir whose chairman was the wife of Baron Perfall, Intendant of the Munich Opera. But try as he might, he remained very much the third conductor. He was young, and headstrong; and, as he later confessed, very much lacked the 'routine', that comes from years of experience in tackling unfamiliar works, in which his colleagues, though less talented than himself, were expert. His tempi were original, and the

Right: Richard Strauss conducting. Caricature by E. Grützner which emphasises Strauss's high forehead, already balding in his twenties

Below: The old Weimar theatre as it was in Strauss's time. (It has since been rebuilt)

singers and musicians much preferred the conventional ones to the new-fangled ideas of an upstart. And lastly, and most seriously, he was frankly bored by some of the operas that he was called on to teach to the singers, rehearse and perform.

Then there were his extra-mural activities. His colleagues were understandably jealous when the third conductor was invited to give concerts elsewhere in Germany and abroad, and when his compositions were equally sought after. At the end of 1887 he gave two concerts in Milan with a total of six rehearsals for one programme played twice. It consisted of:

Weber	*Euryanthe* Overture
R. Strauss	Symphony in F minor
Beethoven	*Leonore* No. 1 Overture
Glinka	*Kamarinskaya*
Wagner	*Meistersinger* Prelude Act 1

The scherzo of Strauss's Symphony was encored on both occasions and because of the success of the concerts, the Milan orchestra gave him a silver baton.

In March 1888 Strauss was given complete charge of a new production at Munich; it was Wagner's first youthful opera *Die Feen*. Strauss plunged into the task with great enthusiasm and carried the singers and musicians with him; the thing was clearly going to be a huge success. Levi was ill and away on sick leave, but when Strauss had fully prepared the opera and the first night was less than two weeks away, Fischer took it away from him on the grounds that he was the senior. In fact, Fischer could not allow a subordinate to win the public acclaim which *Die Feen* was so obviously heading for.

A month later Strauss conducted Cornelius's *Barbier von Bagdad* with great success after only one rehearsal, and so demonstrated that whatever happened he was not to be put down. All the time he was writing to Bülow, saying that Munich was 'a dreary, beery bog' where marsh fever was all around him, and he must get out of it. The opportunity came in the middle of 1889.

Strauss was summoned to Bayreuth as a musical assistant for the 1889 season, and especially as assistant to Perfall on the production of *Parsifal*. There were eight musical assistants that season (one of whom was Humperdinck) and there were to be nine performances of *Parsifal*, four of *Tristan* and five of *Die Meistersinger*. So in being engaged for *Parsifal*, Strauss had one of the more important assignations.

But Bayreuth is only a seasonal appointment and Strauss left there to go to Weimar. Liszt had very recently retired, and the energetic and pleasant Eduard Lassen needed a Kappelmeister to assist him. Strauss joined him on 1 October as Third Grand Ducal Kappelmeister. On 5 October, he conducted his first *Lohengrin* there, as he says: 'with the greatest enthusiasm, and altogether I managed a very nice performance of it'. He found the orchestra very good and accommodating, and the chorus good as well, though 'tiny'.

Strauss's ability as a composer as well as conductor had counted in his favour with the Weimar selection board. On 11 November 1889, Strauss vindicated their choice with the concert première of his *Don Juan*. In fact he had already played it on the piano for Lassen and Bronsart, the theatre's director, and they had been so impressed that they had urged him to give the première in Weimar and nowhere else. Strauss had ample rehearsal for this major event and time to judge whether his orchestration, which he knew to be fiendishly difficult, was in fact playable. The first horn-player called out to him at an early rehearsal: 'Good God! What have we done to you to deserve such punishment'? Strauss later confessed that he had been sorry for the horns and trumpets, but the orchestra responded nobly, and undertook their baptism with him with great good humour. In fact with this work they helped him to launch himself as Germany's outstanding composer.

Over the next three years Strauss suffered from several bouts of illness, one of them serious enough for the doctors to fear for his life. This was partly due to his somewhat sickly health, but more likely to over-work. As well as composing avidly, he was now travelling about a great deal, conducting in places as far distant as Berlin, Frankfurt-am-Main, Eisenach, Amsterdam and Heidelberg. This would not have been possible without Germany's excellent railways. Part of the Kaiser's preparations for the Franco-Prussian War had been to extend and improve the German railway system for the prime need of supply as far West as possible. Now that the railways were built, they offered the most excellent, comfortable and reliable service all over Germany and they suited Strauss admirably.

Weimar proved a beneficial experience to Strauss. Under the friendly and guiding eyes of Lassen and Bronsart, he learned to spend more time than he had done in Munich in getting to enjoy those operas which he did not immediately respond to. His conducting technique was lavish. Since he was a tall and very thin man the slightest movement from the waist was amplified so that he produced results that were often more dramatic than he intended, which outrageously contravened Point 2 of his own admirable advice to young conductors. Just how exhausting an experience it was to watch the young Strauss conducting can be guessed from the comments of Romain Rolland.

22 January, 1898. Richard Strauss concert at Lamoureux's. A young man, tall and thin, curly hair with a tonsure which begins at the crown of the head, a fair moustache, pale eyes and face. Less the head of a musician than that of any provincial young squire . . . He conducts waywardly, abruptly, dramatically, in the same style as Wagner . . . It was enough to see him at the end of the Beethoven Symphony, his great body twisted askew as if struck by both hemiplegia and St Vitus's dance at the same time, his fists clenched and contorted, knock-kneed, tapping with his foot on the dais. . . .

Strauss himself was aware of the fault and as he grew older cultivated a profound distaste for the over-dramatic style.

It is decisive for the technique of conducting that the shorter the movements of the arm, and the more confined to the wrist, then the more precise is the execution. If the arm is allowed to be involved in conducting—which results in a kind of lever-action the effects of which are incalculable—the orchestra is apt to be paralysed and misdirected, unless it is determined from the start (and this is frequently the case with conductors whose down-beat is imprecise) to play according to its own judgement in tacit agreement, as it were, without paying too much attention to the antics of the conductor. The left hand has nothing to do with conducting. Its proper place is in the waistcoat pocket from which it should only emerge to restrain or to make some minor gesture for which in any case a scarcely perceptible glance would suffice. It is better to conduct with the ear instead of with the arm: the rest follows automatically.

In fifty years of practice I have discovered how unimportant it is to mark each crotchet or quaver. What is decisive is that the up-beat, which contains the whole of the tempo which follows, should be rhythmically exact and that the down-beat should be extremely precise. The second half of the bar is immaterial. I frequently conduct it like an *alle breve*.

Above: Strauss and the Berlin Philharmonic orchestra (about 1894).

Right: The front of the National Theatre in Munich before its destruction.

Second-rate conductors are frequently inclined to pay too much attention to the elaboration of rhythmic detail, thus overlooking the proper impressive rendering of the phrase as a whole, and the insinuating lilt of the melody as a whole, which should always be grasped by the listener as a uniform structure. Any modification of tempo made necessary by the character of a phrase should be carried out imperceptibly so that the unity of tempo remains intact.

In 1890, machinations within the Berlin Philharmonic Orchestra affected Strauss when he was approached at Weimar by one of the Berlin management to conduct a series in the 1890/1 season. The invitation was rather late, and for some reason—this part of the correspondence has not survived—von Bülow, then the Philharmonic's conductor, became suspicious of Strauss's intentions, though the latter was entirely blameless and accepted the offer with delight. Bülow's position in Berlin should have been completely secure since he was a superb conductor and musician, but the streak of bitterness in him which Wagner had put there, became more and more obvious as he got older, and when Strauss appeared as if to challenge him, Bülow took it all the wrong way.

Strauss's attachment as guest conductor to the Berlin Philharmonic Concerts was not a success. Now in close touch with peerless musicians, he found them a good deal more demanding and critical and impatient than any of those which he, as a young conductor, had had to face before. It was useful, though very uncomfortable as an experience, and it came a shade too early in his career. There were two great advantages, nevertheless. It brought Strauss before the audience in the Imperial capital, and it brought his own compositions there too, usually in the Berlin Philharmonic 'Popular' matinées.

But there were compensations for this initial failure in Berlin. Strauss's life-long ambition to conduct *Tristan und Isolde* was shortly to be fulfilled in Weimar. It was Strauss's ultimate in all opera, even including Mozart's, and he sought and gained permission from Lassen to prepare and mount his own production of it. *Tristan* had first been heard in Munich under Bülow's baton in 1865 (on the day before Strauss's first birthday), and then, because of its complexities, immoralities and difficulties for all concerned, not again until Lassen gave it in Weimar in 1874. The inspiration which Strauss had from associating with Lassen and with Cosima Wagner during his preparation of the work for his 1891 production was a great fillip to his ambitions. He treated it as a chamber opera, with the orchestra not so much carrying the singers along as allowing them to achieve their vocal climaxes with complete clarity. Cosima Wagner completely endorsed this interpretation of the score.

While this was going on, Strauss continued to bring out his new tone poems, and to play them fairly frequently in Weimar. One programme there in February 1891 consisted of *Macbeth*, *Don Juan* and *Tod und Verklärung*. In the following month the first performance of *Don Juan* in Amsterdam was given by Willem Kes and his Concertgebouw Orchestra. This event was later to help Strauss considerably, for it was the first real Strauss 'break-through' in Holland.

Strauss's health suffered its worst breakdown at this time but he returned to Weimar at the end of 1893 with his opera, *Guntram* completed. He saw Bülow in Berlin in January 1894, for the last time, their friendship had recovered from the suspicions of Berlin and Bülow's support had been immensely valuable to Strauss. He urged his friend, also extremely ill, to go to Cairo to recuperate. Bülow took the advice but too late, he sailed to Egypt but died on arrival. It was a great blow to Strauss, for he had always counted on him for advice and help, and it is fair to say that there was nobody who did so much to shape Strauss's destiny as a conductor. Although Strauss did not always take Bülow's advice there was no offence meant and it is interesting to reflect that Bülow was the partner in two important sets of correspondence: one with Richard Wagner, the other with Richard Strauss.

With Bülow's death, there was now a vacancy among the conductors of the Berlin Philharmonic Concerts, and to his great delight and, one wonders, with how much advance preparation from Bülow—Strauss was invited to return there as guest conductor.

1894 proved to be a most important year. Strauss conducted the world première of his first opera *Guntram* at Weimar in May, a performance which lasted for more than four and a quarter hours, including intervals. But it was too consciously post-Wagnerian in concept, too long-winded and too arduous for the singers. Strauss professed himself satisfied with it for what it was, and he recognized the

Two studies of Strauss conducting. These demonstrate the extravagant movements which were a feature of his style at the beginning of his career.

Franz Schalk (1863–1931). Conductor and director of the Vienna Opera. He was one of Strauss's worst enemies.

fact that he must seek a new direction and not try any more to build upon Wagner.

And now Munich wanted him back, rather on his own terms than on theirs. Strauss could not refuse. Again Bayreuth was a pleasant intervention between appointments and this time he conducted *Tannhäuser* with his fiancée Pauline de Ahna singing Elisabeth, just as she had sung the heroine Freihild in *Guntram*. Siegfried Wagner, Richard Wagner's heir, was one of the musical assistants at Bayreuth that season, and Isadora Duncan was the principal dancer. Cosima Wagner was delighted with Strauss's achievements. 'My word'! she said, 'He's so modern, yet he conducts *Tannhäuser* so well'!

Immediately after Bayreuth and before he took up his appointment on 1 October, Strauss gave a cycle of Mozart operas in Munich and also, with great delight, conducted two performances of *Tristan* there in the very house where it was first heard. This time though, he used the full orchestration. With the Munich Opera appointment went the conductorship of the Munich Akademie Concerts at the Odeon.

Hermann Levi was General Music Director in Munich, and of course knew Strauss's work intimately, not only from his previous time there, but also from working with him at Bayreuth. The Intendant, Ernst von Possart, fancied himself as an actor, and very soon Strauss was to help to satisfy his performing desires. At first Strauss's relationship with theatre management was excellent but soon his European fame and popularity helped to focus unfair jealousies and intrigues against him.

Like a man who had fathered a deformed child, Strauss was determined to justify the existence of his opera *Guntram* against all advice, especially as it had failed at Weimar. In 1895 he again bought out the Weimar production, in Munich. But it was doomed from the start. For the last time in her life, Pauline Strauss de Ahna appeared on the opera stage, as Freihild, in the role she had created, but the revival was disastrous. Strauss never forgave the critics for the way they had treated *Guntram*, and in a mood of wry humour he erected a gravestone to *Guntram*, 'horribly slain by the symphony orchestra of his own father'!

From the winter of 1895, Strauss's tours multiplied, and included Switzerland, Hungary, Russia and England. He also began to champion Gustav Mahler, almost his contemporary. Mahler later gave Strauss's operas whenever possible, in Vienna. In 1897 Strauss visited Paris for the first time and gave a Colonne Concert in which he included his *Tod und Verklärung*. In early April he was engaged with von Possart to give duo concerts of a new composition which Strauss had written especially for them both, a setting for piano and narrator of Tennyson's moving poem, *Enoch Arden*. They planned visits on consecutive days to Stuttgart, Frankfurt-am-Main, Würzburg and Nuremburg. Whether the tour was planned to continue is not known, but it ended there after the birth of Strauss' only child on the day that he and Possart were in Frankfurt.

Willem Mengelberg, at the early age of twenty-four took over the Amsterdam Concertgebouw, and started a Strauss cult there. The Amsterdam Concertgebouw showed their friendliness to Strauss the composer, after getting to know all his tone poems to date, by inviting him to conduct them for the first time in October 1897. But it was far from being the success that they had hoped, in fact they were of the opinion that 'Strauss couldn't conduct'. His programme was varied, and consisted of Berlioz' *King Lear* Overture, Beethoven's Seventh Symphony, Wagner's *Faust* Overture, the *Siegfried Idyll*, and his own *Tod und Verklärung*. Nor was his second concert any more successful four days later, when he gave *Tod und Verklärung* again, Beethoven's *Eroica* Symphony, Mozart's *Eine Kleine* Nachtmusik, and his *Don Juan*. Another conducting tour embracing the Queen's Hall, London, Brussels and Paris ended the year, and in early 1898 he went off again to Paris and then to Madrid.

Don Quixote, Strauss's latest and most advanced tone poem came out in March in Cologne, not Munich, another cause of embitterment to his superiors there. Strauss left the conducting to one of his champions, Franz Wüllner, and the cello part was taken by Fried. In April Strauss went back to Weimar, where he was always welcome, and gave a concert for the Widows and Orphans of the Hofkappelle, the first instance when he showed extreme generosity in this direction. Strauss's four-year contract was now due to expire in six months' time, and Possart was anxious to hold him to Munich. During protracted negotiations, Strauss was offered a life appointment there, but did not jump at it. In October, he gave more performances of *Enoch Arden* with Possart, and returned to Amsterdam, gave *Also sprach Zarathustra*, and was accepted there with honours. It was only his style of conducting that had put them off before. When they understood the results he was able to achieve, they realized that they had grossly underestimated him.

But then came a call from Berlin. Felix Weingartner had left there to go to Vienna, and as usual another general post was about to begin among the top conductors in Germany. Strauss was offered—and accepted—the position of First Kappelmeister in the Royal Prussian Court for a ten years' appointment. He had no regrets at so doing because at the last moment, Perfall in Munich was trying to arrange a salary at a lesser sum than had been discussed. Strauss's stipend in Berlin was 18,000 DM a year, and in addition to his earnings from conducting elsewhere and from his compositions he was now well-off and in the top rank of conductors. He was moreover in a position to influence German music from its capital, from now and until 1918. At the age of thirty-four, he was outstandingly placed as a conductor. Even without his talent as a composer, his future as an international musician and as Germany's most interesting and promising musical personality was secure. The Strausses moved into a comfortable and suitable apartment at 30, Knesebeckerstrasse.

His first appearance on the rostrum of the Royal Prussian Opera was four days after his official appointment, on 5 November 1898, when he conducted a performance of his beloved *Tristan und Isolde*. He followed *Tristan*, three days later, with *Carmen*; then another three days after he gave *Hänsel und Gretel*, and completed his first month's work with Nicolai's *Merry Wives of Windsor*, Auber's *Stumme von Portici*, *Fidelio* and *Rienzi*. Quite clearly this must have entailed an enormous amount of preparation, even given the fact that Strauss was familiar with all these seven (very diverse) operas. In the eight months of the 1898–9 Berlin Opera season he had conducted seventy-one performances of twenty-five different operas and had included two premières, Chabrier's *Brisëis* and Le Borne's *Mudarra*, both of which can be said to have faded from the scene. Strauss finished his season with a complete *Ring* cycle. This kind of pressure was

Right: Drawing by Alois Klob showing Strauss conducting in 1926, with fairly spare gestures and an extremely short baton.

Left: Sketch by Robert Fuchs of the aged Strauss conducting, with very spare gesture (compare picture on page 18).

kept up until the end of the 1901–2 season when, in all, he had conducted 326 performances at the Opera in thirty-seven working months: almost nine performances a month over four years. Until the end of his tenure as Kappelmeister in 1910, Strauss appeared seven hundred times in twelve seasons when, at the age of forty-six, he was undoubtedly the most sought-after conductor in Europe. In addition to all this he had composed three major operas of his own: *Feuersnot*, *Salome* and *Elektra*.

The Berlin engagement also established Strauss firmly as chief conductor of the Berlin Philharmonic Concerts which were given annually between October and February in an important and special series of ten concerts in the old Philharmonic Hall. Not only was Strauss able to introduce his own works into programmes, to air new compositions by other composers, but also to indulge in his favourite works by Mozart, Beethoven and Brahms. With all this went the obligation to play new works by his superiors in Berlin, like the Intendant, Bolko von Hoffberg's Symphony and Max von Schillings' extract from *Moloch*. Strauss conducted the Berlin Philharmonic Concerts regularly, right through the First World War and up to the beginning of 1920; in view of the fierce nationalism which gripped Europe during the period of the First World War, it is hardly surprising that Strauss's pro-

Overleaf: Strauss taking a rehearsal in the Grosses-musikvereinsaal, Vienna.

grammes were mainly confined to German composers. Berlioz is the sole representative of French music; Verdi never occurs once; and the only British composer is Percy Grainger, whose *Mock Morris* was given to a surprised and delighted Philharmonic audience at a matinée concert in February 1914, immediately preceding Beethoven's Fifth Symphony.

As he grew older, Strauss tended to arrive, if not a moment or two late, right on time on the rostrum, barely acknowledge the applause, and launch himself into the opening bars. The last act of whichever familiar work it was, tended to go briskly so that there might be that extra hand of Skat afterwards! Yet so professionally were the tempi pushed, that hardly anybody was aware of the difference. One might raise the eyebrows at such behaviour, but Strauss lived to a great age and became increasingly disenchanted with the bulk of the operatic repertoire, including his own works. Apart from Mozart's operas, Beethoven's *Fidelio*, *Tristan* and most of Wagner's operas, he was not able to sustain his interest in the rest. In about 1940 (when he was seventy-six) he wrote: 'I suppose I have heard *Parsifal* and *Der Ring* fifty times each (usually when I myself have been rehearsing and conducting) yet I cannot have enough of the revelations of this orchestra and I discover in it new beauties and am grateful for new revelations every time'.

Strauss's contract in Berlin was due to expire in 1918, and although he was prepared to continue there, in a mode of existence which suited him very well, he was unable to agree with the opera director Count Georg von Hülsen-Haeseler, a Prussian of the old school and brother of the chief of the Kaiser's military cabinet. Hülsen-Haeseler wanted to 'soften' and revise a great deal of the text of *Der Rosenkavalier* before its Berlin première in 1911 and came up against violent objections from both Strauss and Hofmannsthal. All the same he kept to his alterations. Accordingly, when Strauss was offered a post at Vienna, the only one he could take without losing international status, he accepted readily. He left Berlin's Court Opera in May 1918; but in the turmoil caused by the overthrow of the imperial house after the war he returned almost at once on a purely caretaker basis, in October, staying there until the autumn of 1919, (Hülsen-Haeseler having resigned in November 1918).

The Vienna appointment placed him in co-directorship with Franz Schalk, his former colleague at the Berlin Opera and a conductor of some merit. Schalk had directed the first performances of the second version of *Ariadne* and *Die Frau ohne Schatten* in Vienna, where he had worked from 1900 as a conductor, and since 1918 as director. But it was not a happy partnership. No directorship of the Vienna Opera ever seems to be. Since Mahler's time, the intrigues and petty politics have made the director's tenure of short duration, and Schalk and Strauss were, in any case, incompatible.

Strauss continued with a wide range of outside engagements of which his tour of South America with the Vienna Philharmonic Orchestra counted as being for Vienna. But in his absence a good deal of intriguing went on against him, not only because he was a Bavarian and therefore a 'foreigner' but also because he had emphasized the production of his own operas there, quite out of proportion, it was felt, to their true weight in the scheme of things. Also his antipathy to Schalk led to a personal feud, and Strauss saw that, as in the case of Gustav Mahler, it would be preferable to work for the Vienna Opera from outside. So he left there in the summer of 1924 after only four years. In a very short time all was forgiven, and he established a very good relationship with the city, living in his exquisite house in Belvedere, on and off, for the rest of his active life.

Strauss and Schalk had taken the Vienna State Opera to Argentina on a good-will mission in 1923. He was there for the whole time, but Schalk only stayed for three weeks. Strauss has recorded details of programmes they had on this tour: 'My first stay in Buenos Aires was most pleasant . . . I obtained very good performances of *Salome* and *Elektra* . . . Just imagine how hard the people work here: Thursday afternoon *Generalprobe* of *Elektra*, Friday *Elektra*. High point of the work, Sunday afternoon performance of *Salome*, and *Elektra* in the evening, both under my own direction, in which, as it happened, Frau Dahmen sang an outstanding Salome in the afternoon and Chrysothemis in the evening. And both were good performances'. This may have been hard work and unwise of the redoubtable Frau Dahmen, but what about the taxing of Strauss's own strength, at the age of sixty, of which there is no mention!

After his departure from Vienna, Strauss

Above: Portrait of Strauss by Professor Schuntzer, made just before the First World War.

Left: Strauss conducting a rehearsal at Bayreuth in 1933.

maintained a satisfactory relationship with the opera house so that he went back as guest conductor once the hubbub had died down. Ever afterwards he remained a freelance conductor, so much in demand that he had far more requests than he could accommodate, and was thus in the happy position of being able to choose.

It was in the 1920s too, that his concert repertory began to be limited to Mozart, Beethoven, Liszt, Wagner and his own works at home; and abroad to Bruckner, Mahler, Reger, Pfitzner and Strauss when they were new works. He never lost an opportunity of exporting modern German music.

For a while during his critical year of political ostracism (1935–6) under the Third Reich, Strauss maintained his reputation as a conductor by going abroad to Italy, Belgium and France, and by giving one opera performance (*Ariadne*) at Covent Garden in 1936. After the Second World War he returned to London, thanks to the efforts of Sir Thomas Beecham, and appeared in some memorable concerts at the Albert Hall. The almost immobile veteran controlled two London Orchestras of 1947 so differently from Beecham, Toscanini, Sir Henry Wood and others, that many of the players said, as had been said before in Berlin and Amsterdam, 'He couldn't conduct. He didn't do anything'. By then, perhaps, the old dynamism was waning, but those at the front desks were still aware of it.

The last time he ever conducted in the opera house was in Munich in 1949, the day before his eighty-fifth birthday, when he took over the baton from Karl Böhm and managed to direct the finales of Acts II and III of *Der Rosenkavalier* at the Dress Rehearsal. And the last time he ever stood in front of an orchestra was when he conducted the 'Moonlight' interlude from *Capriccio* with the Bavarian Radio Orchestra in their studio on July 13th of the same year. As he himself said, 'Conducting is, after all, a difficult business. One has to be seventy years of age to realise this fully'!

Right: The Benedictine Monastery at Ettal, near Garmisch. Strauss sent his son and one of his grandsons to the school in the monastery and was writing an opera for the boys (The Donkey's Shadow) *which remained unfinished at his death.*

Overleaf: Painting of Cortina D'Ampezzo by Rudolf von Alt, where the Strausses used to spend their holidays when Richard was a boy. (The painting is in the Albertina in Vienna).

Chapter 3

Strauss and his Wife

Strauss and his wife Pauline de Ahna. A less apprehensive picture of Strauss than the one on page 43, but one which shows the balance of the marital relationship.

More than most composers, Strauss had cause to be thankful to his wife for her eager devotion to him and to his work. That the degree of this devotion was of a kind that would be intolerable to many men and positively murderous to the majority of artists is not entirely to the point. For Pauline Strauss de Ahna was an indomitable woman, Richard Strauss was a mild and amiable man, and they loved each other deeply. Had they not loved each other—even though there were times when his affection faltered—there is plenty of evidence to suggest that Strauss may not have had sufficient strength of purpose to apply himself to composition as industriously as he did. As it turned out, his wife used to wait, watch and listen while he was at work, just in case he shirked the job on hand and tried to get up and go for a walk. This would have wasted precious time, and she would not countenance it.

She was the second eldest daughter of a Bavarian General and belonged to a much higher social class than Strauss, whose brewing mother and horn-playing father were counted as very middle class. The de Ahnas were of an old and honourable family connected with the Army, and fervent Bavarian patriots. What made it possible for Strauss to associate with them from the start was the old General's passion for music. Pauline had graduated from the Munich Conservatoire as a singer in 1886, but had not been offered an engagement by any impresario or management. Her father had a reasonable baritone voice and used to give amateur recitals locally, when his favourite show-piece was Wolfram's song to the evening star from *Tannhäuser*. Consequently such an inherently musical family could be expected to waive social taboo if it wished to cultivate a man who, like Richard Strauss, had begun to distinguish himself in musical Germany. Happily Strauss was also socially *au fait*, charming and handsome, in the style of the times.

In August 1887 Strauss visited his Uncle George Pschorr, his mother's brother, in the village of Feldafing, to the southwest of Munich, and through him met the de Ahnas. They were intrigued by the precocious young man (he was 23), for they had already heard a good deal about him. And so they accepted him socially without demur. Pauline became his singing pupil, and an instant and mutual attraction developed—the more interesting in the light of the authority which she was to exercise over him later.

Certainly Strauss's work was greatly influenced by his love for Pauline de Ahna. Indeed, his first really successful work was *Don Juan*, a symphonic poem based on an unusual but nevertheless erotic version of the legend by the German poet von Lenau. To describe the work as successful would be to use a half-hearted word for the enormous *éclat* which it received. At the time when Strauss met Pauline de Ahna he had had at least one known affair. It was with Dora Wihan, the wife of a cellist in the Munich Opera Orchestra; and from what was clearly a large correspondence, only one letter—from Strauss to Dora—has survived. Strauss's father knew all about the romance (there are no secrets in orchestras) and in a letter cautioned his son about the dangers of women, and, more especially, when he was conducting female choruses. But Strauss was not a sensual man, and his finding Pauline was the normal procedure of a combination of chance with a man looking for a wife. Whenever he was able, during his time at Munich, he visited her at Feldafing and, from 1891 spent holidays with her and her family at Marquartstein. 'Summer at Marquartstein' began to figure prominently in his diary.

When he obtained the appointment at Weimar with von Bülow in 1888, Strauss was too far from Munich and Feldafing to see Pauline often enough so, with von Bülow's support, he arranged for her to join the opera company in Weimar and be with him. Possibly she inspired that first, though unsuccessful, opera *Guntram*.

Pauline arrived at Weimar in October 1890, was heard there by Cosima Wagner, and was cast as Elisabeth in the first Bayreuth production of *Tannhäuser* in 1891. Then, as now, the Wagner family cast their productions by listening to singers performing, and judged their own requirements without the artificial and uncomfortable expedient of auditions. Pauline satisfied Cosima Wagner completely, and the old lady decided that she would find out more about her, and also more about Richard Strauss, for she could do with men like him at Bayreuth.

She had been running the Festspielhaus since her husband Richard's death in February 1883. In 1891 she invited Pauline and Richard Strauss to spend Christmas with her at the family home at Wahnfried. Richard Strauss was an ideal candidate for Bayreuth, and Cosima half hoped to see this sensible, talented and altogether eligible young man as her son-in-law. Strauss was at that time preparing for a life's ambition, his own production of *Tristan und Isolde* at Weimar, and was delighted to find Cosima more than helpful—she even allowed him to consult Wagner's manuscript score and notes. So far as Cosima was concerned, Pauline de Ahna was an obstruction to her plans, but she had not reckoned with a personality just as determined as her own. Cosima lost in her efforts to win Strauss as a husband for her daughter and there was no further professional connection between her and the Strausses. Indeed Pauline de Ahna was never invited back to Bayreuth after her marriage to Strauss in 1894. Yet the families remained on friendly social terms and Cosima sent Pauline an amusing telegram on the birth of her son in 1897, offering to be his governess but imploring them both not to have Zarathustra as his tutor.

Strauss was very ill in 1892 and had an enforced and solitary convalescence abroad. On his recovery he returned to Weimar in June 1893 with *Guntram* almost completely scored and with Pauline in mind to sing the soprano lead. He finished the opera in Marquartstein during an idyllic summer, and then returned with Pauline to Weimar for the 1893–4 season. On May 10th, during the *Generalprobe* (or final dress rehearsal) of *Guntram*, an event took place which illustrates the highly volatile disposition of the lady whom Strauss was to marry. It is also the first of a whole host of anecdotes about her which persisted until late on in her life.

The de Ahna's country house at Marquartstein, where Strauss did much of his courting.

Strauss, on the conductor's rostrum, was giving his notes to the cast at the end of the rehearsal but seemed to have no comments for Pauline. Either because she thought he was being far too kind to her or she felt left out of the proceedings, she suddenly threw her vocal score (a large and heavy volume) at Strauss's head, screaming out that she too wanted his criticisms. She then stormed off the stage to her dressing-room. Strauss followed her. Loud cries of anger were heard proceeding from back-stage and the leader of the orchestra and several players made up a deputation in case there was need for them to rescue their beloved conductor from this savage Bavarian soprano. However when the leader put his head round the door and said that the orchestra preferred in future not to work with her, Strauss smiled and replied: 'I'm sorry you should think that necessary. I must inform you that Fräulein de Ahna has just accepted my proposal of marriage'.

On 10 September 1894, Pauline and Richard

were married in Weimar. His wedding present to her was the enchanting set of four love songs, Op. 27: *Ruhe meine Seele*, *Cäcilie*, *Heimliche Aufforderung* and *Morgen*! Each expresses a different facet of his love for her through three poets, Karl Henckell, Julius Hart and John Henry Mackay. But with their marriage Pauline took charge. Strauss for his part accepted her domination of their domestic relationship as not only good for him but indispensible in ensuring that he work the number of hours which she had prescribed. From his own letters home from Egypt which he sent his parents while convalescing there, Strauss gave details of his working day:-

8 am.	Get up and have breakfast. Stroll for half an hour by the Nile.
10–1	Work.
1 pm.	Luncheon. Read or play cards.
3–4	Work.
4 pm.	Tea. Walk until 6 pm. 'when I do my duty in admiring the usual sunset'.
6–7	Work again or write letters.
7 pm.	Dinner. After it chat and smoke until 9.30 pm.
10 pm.	To bed.

This timetable gives Strauss, at the most, five hours work which, combined with the somewhat casual attitudes expressed by the words 'stroll' and 'chat' that are altogether characteristic of his easy-going nature, clearly needed tightening up. The fact that it *was* a regular timetable and not haphazard pleased Pauline, but she modified it considerably when he returned home. Immediately after breakfast she issued the order: '*Richard jetzt gehst componieren*'! ('Now Richard, off you go and compose') and off he went obediently to his study to concentrate hard on whatever was on hand at the moment. At lunchtime he had a little respite, and afterwards, perhaps, a walk in the garden (but a *walk* and not a *stroll*) before he was driven back to his study to continue.

Pauline was up against a powerful opponent to work in the card game of skat. Strauss once said that he had two lives, one was as a composer, the other as a conductor. In truth he had three lives and the third—just as important to him as the other two—was as a first-class skat player—one of Germany's most outstanding. Pauline did not play skat, it was a man's game by tradition, nor was she at all happy about the

Strauss and his wife on a picnic with Max Schillings, (the composer and conductor) and a friend.

laughter and shouting from the card room—as at the Generalprobe of *Guntram*, she did not like to be left out. But she tolerated it as a reasonable relaxation for her husband and, better still, a relaxation away from other women. Skat was so important to Strauss that wherever he might be another three players were got together or forced together to make up the required four. In places as far removed from Munich as London, Barcelona or Constantinople, three players always materialized to meet the maestro after the opera was over. When Strauss went to Bayreuth in 1933 members of the resident orchestra were detailed off to play. But they complained to Winifred Wagner that they could not afford to play against Strauss since he always won. To placate the guest conductor the games continued but two musicians had their losses made good by the Festival management each morning.

Pauline and Richard had one child Franz Alexander, who was born on 12 April 1897. Pauline was completely composed and entirely prepared for the event, even though twins were forecast. Strauss went away on a short tour with his melodrama *Enoch Arden*, with himself at the piano and Ernst von Possart as the narrator. Pauline had a difficult, even dangerous confinement and was obliged, much against her will, to have an anaesthetic. In a letter to his parents four days later, Strauss told them that she had 'nobly upheld her profession of house-wife'. On coming round from the anaesthetic, she immediately asked the doctor whether he would care for a cognac.

Such was Strauss's contentment with his wife and son and their family life, that he thrice portrayed them all in major compositions. The fact that there was never another child may have been due to Pauline's difficult confinement; or it may, as she claimed have been

Strauss's house in the Belvedere, Vienna which he built on ground given to him by the grateful corporation for his work at the Opera.

her husband's responsibility. At a party in Vienna many years later, she was heard to exclaim in a loud voice: 'Another child! Good heavens, you don't know what trouble I had in getting him to start this one'! Extravagant statements aimed at shocking convention were entirely in character from Pauline, but whether or not this one was true is by the nature of things difficult to determine. Strauss dearly loved his son, but may well have shrunk from the prospect of a large family. His sex life as such, does not seem to have been particularly active and certainly there is no evidence after the marriage that Strauss ever philandered, which paradoxically seemed to have annoyed Pauline. An utterly faithful husband robbed her of one major excuse for recriminations and domestic tantrums.

This aspect of their lives is treated openly and comically in the opera *Intermezzo*. The two main characters are Herr Storch, an opera conductor (Strauss), Frau Storch (Pauline) and 'Bubi', their child. When the work was first given at Dresden in 1924 the two principal singers wore masks representing himself and Pauline—much to Strauss's surprise and secret pleasure. The plot hinges on misunderstanding. An invitation by a friend of Storch to a certain Mitzi Maier (of doubtful virtue) depends on her asking for a ticket. When she gets the name wrong and addresses an intimate note to Herr Kappelmeister Robert Storch, he is away from home and his jealously disposed wife opens the envelope. This—or something very like it—once happened to Strauss in 1907, when his name was confused with that of a Herr Stransky. Pauline was exceedingly angry, threatened divorce, called the lawyer, and only when the mistake was explained to her did she very reluctantly *forgive* her husband!

Remembering these events all too well, Strauss transferred them in exact detail to

Cast of the première of Intermezzo *showing Lotte Lehmann as Christine, discussing a fine point with Strauss who is holding the score. Behind Lotte Lehmann is Josef Correck who played the part of Robert Storch, in discussion with the designer, Lothar Wallerstein.*

Above: An informal and unlikely picture of Strauss on a sledge at St Moritz, being closely observed by a gentleman dressed very elegantly for the occasion.

Left: Gustav Mahler (1860–1911). The composer and great musical architect of the Vienna Opera. A contemporary and friend of Strauss

Intermezzo, together with another character, in the opera called Baron Lummer, who had once tried to borrow money from Pauline while Strauss was away from home. The opera was intended by Strauss to take its place among his various stage-cum-musical portraits of his wife. He wanted to 'compose' her over and over again because he found her quite as interesting and certainly more surprising in her behaviour than any of the quasi-goddesses or the demi-spirits conjured up by his librettist Hofmannsthal. For his part Hofmannsthal was disgusted at such a bourgeois idea as *Intermezzo*, and 'bourgeois' is just the word that Strauss used to describe it. At one time he found himself in need of help with the libretto and sought it from the Salzburg writer Hermann Bahr. He soon advised the composer to try and work it all out for himself, since only he knew everything there was to know about his heroine. Bahr, moreover, was worried by the direct way in which Strauss was intending to portray Pauline, and as he and Pauline did not get on in any case, he edged his way out of what was already becoming an awkward situation.

Intermezzo has, in fact, a very important place in Strauss's output. It shows him composing in an entirely new manner after his first temporary release from Hofmannsthal (between *Die Frau ohne Schatten* and *Die Aegyptische Helena*) after a partnership of over 13 years. His use of natural speech-sounds to create a sung line of great sensitivity and meaning is the second significant aspect of this opera. This vocal line is of necessity dependent, for all intelligibility to an audience, on the orchestral texture being carefully balanced. Strauss wrote a fascinating preface on the subject of vocal and orchestral balance in the full score of *Intermezzo* which contains much valuable information for anybody who is trying to convey speech to an audience, whether with musical accompaniment or not. It also offers advice to conductors on how to moderate their accompaniment to singers so that the all-important words get across.

Intermezzo is built on a series of scenes rather than in corporate acts and it is interesting to find that at this same time, both Hindemith and Alban Berg were experimenting with the same idea. It certainly makes for a fast-flowing sequence and assists the action enormously. Each scene of *Intermezzo* is so tautly constructed and the whole is so perfectly adapted to the theatre, that the director Max Reinhardt once told Strauss that he would willingly produce *Intermezzo* as a play without a note of music.

There is an amusing scene that concerns winter sports which of course Strauss took from real life. He and Pauline used to go to St Moritz during the winter seasons, and the picture shown on page 35 will prove the point. This was the exception rather than the rule while the Strauss's were up in the mountains, but they used to enjoy this kind of relaxation. The winter season of 1909–10 was particularly sunny. Frau Strauss wrote to a friend that she and her husband were taken for coloured people when they reached Dresden for the *Rosenkavalier* rehearsals.

At the first performance of *Intermezzo* in Dresden Lotte Lehmann was engaged to sing Frau Storch, almost certainly because her voice, according to contemporaries still living, was of all soprano voices of the time, nearest to Pauline de Ahna's. Here was yet another effort to achieve complete—and cruel—reality in bringing the Strauss's private life onto the opera stage. Pauline professed to be pleased with *Intermezzo*, yet one can only be utterly perplexed about the whole business since it is all directed so obviously against her; or so it seems. One of the characters describes Frau Storch as 'absolutely terrible' (*einfach fechterlich*) yet Strauss wrote the part. If he was trying to get his own back for the appalling way she sometimes treated him there was no more obvious way to do so than this; but Strauss was not that kind of man and would certainly not stoop to such a mean act. It is all rather difficult to understand.

Nearly a quarter of a century earlier than *Intermezzo*, after the première of *Feuersnot*, we are told that Pauline had refused to speak to him at all, attacking the work in a loud voice and claiming that Strauss had stolen it all from another composer. She made him walk three paces behind her out of the box from which they had watched the performance, to their hotel. 'I shall be sleeping alone tonight' was her husband's comment to a friend. Pauline may have been the spur to prevent Strauss's indolence at home, but she seems too often to have maintained an impossibly domineering attitude in public and especially among their friends and acquaintances.

Gustav and Alma Mahler positively detested her. If they happened to be staying in the same town or village, the Mahlers cringed at the very sight of Pauline Strauss, for she was given to hailing them from a long way off, to the astonishment of passers by. Others still living, who knew her at first hand, still become somewhat strained and prefer to change the subject or simply splutter incoherently about the impossible Frau Strauss. Yet it does seem as though Richard Strauss adored her. She was, he said, his 'real helpmate' the same expression which he uses to describe the Hero's wife in *Ein Heldenleben*.

This tone poem and the *Sinfonia Domestica* had superseded *Intermezzo* as the setting of his family to music. *Ein Heldenleben* (A Hero's Life) Opus 40, was composed in 1897–8 and first performed at Frankfurt-am-Main on 3 March 1899 under Strauss himself. At the party after a London performance of *Heldenleben* a toast was proposed to the composer, whereupon Pauline called out 'No, not Strauss,' (pointing to herself) 'Strauss—de Ahna'! It is the seventh and last of the series of compositions in the mould of the tone poem, unless one considers the *Sinfonia Domestica* as the last tone poem rather than as a symphony in one movement. Likewise the first composition which started this series, *Aus Italien*, is in a symphonic mould, though it is not so described.

In spite of the opposing view of the important Straussian authority Norman Del Mar, I agree with Richard Specht, the German musicologist, who writes in the preface of Eulenberg's miniature score of *Ein Heldenleben*: that the work is 'a defiant confession and portrait of Strauss himself in the form of a symphony'. One may argue as to whether or not the work is a symphony but there can surely be no doubt of its autobiographical aspect. Strauss introduces himself—the hero composer—at the outset, and in the long strides up the scale in triplets, and down again in dotted- and semiquavers (as if to demonstrate his own versatility) we are not so far removed from the entrance of his other self-hero, Don Juan.

Again, in contrasting the feminine themes in these two tone poems, one finds points of resemblance in Frau Strauss's theme to that of the Loved One in *Don Juan*. Both are played on the solo violin *molto espressivo*, both are what have come to be known as 'schmalzy' tunes, both are very feminine. *Ein Heldenleben* has a virtuoso violin part in it which sometimes tends to bring the shape of the work nearer to a kind of composition with obbligato violin for which there is no set name, this I feel, rather than a symphony. All the same, the hint is

Study by the painter Max Liebermann, which depicts a careworn and oppressed Strauss.

Above: An unusual picture of Strauss playing chess, rather than skat, but showing the same concentration.

Opposite above: The opera house Unter den Linden in Berlin. Totally destroyed in World War Two.

Opposite below: George Szell. Hungarian-born conductor and assistant to Strauss, who has left many fine interpretations of the Tone Poems on record.

there, that Strauss the Great Lover of *Don Juan* (and all the tone poems are inescapably autobiographical) is another guise for Strauss the Great Hero with his Wife/Mistress in their transformation from sensual love in *Don Juan* to themselves in *Ein Heldenleben.* All the shrewishness of Frau Strauss is in the spiky solo which she is given and in portraying her like this, Strauss has been no less and no more sparing than in *Intermezzo.*

In Strauss's next domestic composition, the *Sinfonia Domestica*, Opus 53 and composed between 1902–3, the pater familias strides up the scale as before, but not quite as before. At Figure 1 he is not there at the outset: we need preparation this time. His very masculine theme is intended to portray his fiery nature, but beforehand we have heard rapidly descriptive strokes to signify other sides to his nature: expansiveness, dreaminess and a brief indication of his equally short bursts of short-temper. But it is the main theme which is, and which is meant to be, the most significant, and in comparing it with Strauss's earlier appearances in his tone poems one finds that the contours, while familiar, have been smoothed out as if to imply maturity.

Pauline's musical portrait in the *Domestica* is also more mature than those in the two preceding works, for of course she is a mother by this time, far more sedate and glowing.

What is more, the third family theme of 'Bubi' makes its début in the most wild and onomatopoeic manner, as the baby in the bath, as though extending Strauss's boast that he was able to set absolutely anything to music.

This upset the early critics considerably and is still one of the main targets in unfavourable criticisms of the work, even more than Strauss's purposeful taking off (*Ganz der Papa*; *Ganz die Mama*) of silly uncles and aunts as they look dotingly at the small pink object. These are a few of the remaining comments with which Strauss had originally laced his score. He intended to remove them all, but those which he left in, point even more strongly to an originally detailed programme, a fact which he later attempted to conceal altogether.

There is a great deal of beautiful music in the *Domestica*, and it is not played as often as it deserves, possibly on account of the large orchestra it requires. The very clear domestic scenes of quarrel, reconciliation and side issues are based on an all-embracing mood of true love, and the work is easy to understand. The interwoven themes are each based on the family, and it is the family which is the whole root of the work and which gives it its *raison d'être.* Once again certain embarrassment was caused by Strauss's frankness, and this time by a whole audience when it was performed in an American department store. Having partially overcome the extremely personal aspects of the score, which removes a whole wall of the Strauss house to all and sundry, he horrified the New Yorkers even more when, on being criticized for playing in such a place and not in a proper concert hall, he had his reply ready. 'I think it perfectly honourable,' he said, 'for a composer with a wife and child to support, to play his works wherever an audience can be assembled, even if it is in a department store.'

This was after the world première, which had taken place at Carnegie Hall on 21 March 1904, during a Strauss Festival. To those American critics who asked him whether the work was meant to be humorous, Strauss quickly replied that there is nothing *humorous* about one's family, and that the *Sinfonia Domestica* is *serious* music.

Strauss's own sense of humour has, of course, a great deal to do with his attitude to outsiders as well as to his family, and Pauline in particular. This dry humour is one of the most buoyant factors in his music. *Till Eulenspiegel* is the first composition positively to bubble over with it, though previously the *Burleske* for piano and orchestra, as well as the song *Ah, me! Unhappy Man* both demonstrated it strongly. Apart from the domestic compositions which should not, despite Strauss, be taken entirely seriously, there is the rich and sophisticated comedy in *Der Rosenkavalier* and the bucolic fun contained in the Commedia dell'arte part of *Ariadne on Naxos.* Yet of all the brands of humour which Strauss weaves through his compositions, none has the satirical bite to such a degree as the twelve songs called *Krämerspiegel* which he wrote as a demonstration of disgust against German music publishers. With this very significant side to his nature, it is doubtful whether Strauss could have married and lived for so long with a woman if she had not at least a streak of humour in her too. Hofmannsthal was not only an expert judge of character, but was close to the Strausses. He said that he had based the un-

Above: Sketch of Strauss in extreme old age, by Gerda von Stengel.

Opposite: Strauss playing on the piano from his full score of the Festival of Music for the 2,600th Anniversary of the Japanese Empire *at a diplomatic reception for the Japanese in Berlin.*

Below: Dr Ernst Roth (1896–1971), chairman of Messrs Boosey and Hawkes and close friend of the Strausses from immediately after the War. From that time Dr Roth acquired the bulk of publishing rights of Strauss's music and played a large part in rehabilitating the composer in the last years of his life.

sympathetic character of the Dyer's Wife in *The Woman without a Shadow* on Pauline. In a letter to Strauss he wrote: 'she is a *bizarre* woman with a very beautiful soul *au fond*; strange, moody, domineering and yet at the same time likeable; she would in fact be the principal character . . . your wife might well, in all discretion, be taken as a model—that of course is wholly *entre nous* and not of any great importance.' I suggest that it was on the contrary of the greatest importance and that Hofmannsthal disclosed this to Strauss, precisely because he knew how well he 'set' his wife to music. I have extended part of the quotation out of context in the phrase about the principal character (although this comes in the same letter), for of course a person such as Pauline is bound to be a principal character wherever she is—and more especially when she is with her husband. It is interesting to read that Hofmannsthal saw 'a beautiful soul' in Pauline, for he and his wife did not in the least enjoy her company.

When Strauss was at the height of his prestige in Germany, though not at the height of his composing powers, Pauline behaved in exactly the same way towards him and towards everybody else as she had always done. And during the Nazi régime, and especially when Strauss was politically in disfavour, Pauline was extremely rash in what she said and did. Her criticisms never abated. She once declared to Baldur von Schirach, *Gauleiter* of Vienna, that there would 'still be a place for him in Garmisch when the war was lost and the rest of the "shower" in Berlin had been. . . .' The final word was drowned in protest, embarrassed coughs and forced laughter from her audience. Schirach smiled and replied courteously enough that he was grateful to her, but did not think it would come to that. Strauss stood by, mopping his brow, and not for the first time. As events worsened, it became far more sensible for the whole family to stay indoors: for the grandsons and their Jewish mother, for Pauline and her angry tongue. There were always informers anxious to do their bit for the Fatherland. Pauline who was pathologically house proud had always insisted that visitors to the house remove their shoes on entering, but on one occasion when Viorica Ursuleac, wife of Clemens Krauss, called there, she was forbidden entrance altogether because she was wearing a fur coat given to her by Goering. Pauline had a great dislike of Prussians and for her, as for every good Bavarian, everybody in Berlin was 'Prussian'. Their faults ranged from losing the war, to imposing rationing but, worst of all, they were preventing her husband from collecting his royalties, and were making it increasingly difficult for him to work at all. When she railed against Goering in particular, it was pointed out to her that Goering was born in Bavaria. It made no difference, he was still 'an absolutely abominable fellow' to her.

After the war, when the Strausses were eventually allowed to go to Switzerland, Pauline behaved outrageously in the various hotels where they tried to get cheap accommodation. Since the Swiss have no sympathy for patrons without money, Strauss was obliged to accept their insults and to write out scores of his own works to be deposited against the cost of their board and lodging. Some clever Swiss lawyer had evidently anticipated their later worth. The hotel staffs despised the Strausses and despite their intense relief at getting out of Germany, they were wretchedly unhappy and were really at a miserable level of existence. Pauline, especially, made things worse by bossing the servants about in the manner of a *grande dame*, and complaining about the most trivial things. As a result they were asked to move on fairly frequently, and she refused point blank to stay at one hotel because she took an instant dislike to the shape of the legs of a chair in the hall. One can put this down to her autocratic upbringing, to strain, and to frustration, but it fits with her general capriciousness.

Yet when Strauss left Switzerland to fly to London for a month in 1947, Pauline was separated from him for longer than she had been since his visit to South America in 1924. When they were reunited in Montreux, the old couple wept for joy to see each other again, and clasped each other as if they had survived a disaster and had reached a new world. The other world was not far off either. Strauss died on 8 September 1949 of a bladder complaint that might have been forestalled for a while longer had the Nazi authorities not prevented him from going to Switzerland earlier for cures. Pauline, left behind in mental solitude and confusion, died, despite the efforts of her son and daughter-in-law to console her, peacefully at home in Garmisch on 13 May 1950.

Chapter 4

Strauss and the Orchestra

Strauss's output falls into three main categories, so logically related that, when looked at now in retrospect, it appears that up to the end of 1906, he had his career very carefully planned. He was, in any case, a skilful organizer of his work schedule. He knew, with absolute certainty, upon which date he was going to complete and be able to deliver a song or the full score of an opera, and his publishers came to rely on this accuracy when arranging their own engraving and printing schedules. His regular working hours and his confidence in his own ability to create at a constant speed made all this possible and, of course, most convenient for everybody concerned. Sometimes his Muse deserted him; but this did not stop him from turning out his scores on time. They came automatically. 'Note-spinning' was what Frau Strauss deftly though a trifle unkindly called these periods of almost automatic composition. The music came off his pen as if from a loom or a machine; it looked good on the page, the score was as clean as ever, but when played it lacked the sparkle, the originality, the genius that is Strauss at his best. Every artist needs some kind of impetus to send him on his way into a new creation, unless, as with Mozart, the Muse is always obligingly present. Yet even then, fine work only results if there is a strong technique behind the pen, a framework upon which to hang and peg the inspired thoughts, and Strauss possessed this technique to a marked degree. He had only to take one look at the sketch for a composition to see its immediate possibilities for development, sometimes, indeed elaborating and thickening it beyond the needs of the occasion.

The three main groups of Strauss's characteristic and most valuable compositions are the tone-poems, the Lieder (or songs) and the operas. The tone-poems were constructed in a variety of ways, all leading him to facility in the widest possible employment of orchestral forces, including specialist or solo parts for violin, viola and cello. The Lieder familiarized him with writing for the voice, especially the soprano voice, and in setting a great selection of poems, of different moods and metres. From this it seems that Opera was the logical conclusion, and so it fell out. Once Strauss had exhausted the possibilities of the tone-poem, he turned his attention to the opera, yet continued to compose songs intermittently until the end of his life. Of course he composed other kinds of works as well, and in this chapter I shall describe how his career was shaped through his output up to the end of the tone-poems, and we shall look at his achievements in the field of Lieder. But those operas and compositions which he was miraculously able to write in a kind of upsurge at the end of his life, will be left until later.

In his very early composing days, Strauss wrote for the piano. The Five Piano Pieces, Opus 3; the four-movement Piano Sonata in B minor, Opus 5; and the Five 'Voice-Pictures' for Piano, Opus 9 were all composed between 1881–84 and were all that Strauss wrote for solo piano. They are pleasant enough trifles, redolent of such romantics as Mendelssohn or Schumann, with occasional flashes of Beethoven. But they do not tell one who wrote them, there is as yet no sign of any of Strauss's characteristics. He never composed a piano concerto, surprisingly enough, for he was fond of the instrument and played it well. Between 1885–86 he was at work on two compositions that were related to the piano concerto: a cadenza to Mozart's C minor masterpiece, K.491, and his own *Burleske* for piano and orchestra. Strauss made his début in Meiningen with the Mozart Piano Concerto under von Bülow's baton, and the cadenza which he wrote and played on this occasion has been preserved.

Strauss had previously been working on both a *Scherzo* and a *Rhapsody* for piano and

Strauss at home in Garmisch in the mid nineteen-twenties, looking camera-shy and ill-at-ease.

orchestra, but neither of these (disconnected) works materialized. But the *Burleske* is another matter. It is a genial, humorous and very entertaining one-movement piece for virtuoso pianist, solo timpanist and orchestra which last for about 17 minutes—in fact about three or four of these minutes seem too long. Strauss attempted to play the piano part himself in Meiningen, while conducting the run-through, but had to give up this difficult task altogether. Strauss the pianist was unable to cope with what Strauss the composer had given him. It was not until 1890 that Eugen d'Albert (the composer of *Tiefland*) was the soloist in the successful première of the *Burleske*, under Strauss's baton, in Eisenach.

The only other works involving the piano are two recitations with piano accompaniment, which came at the end of the century. They are *Enoch Arden*, Opus 38, with a thematic piano part that constantly reminds the listener of the characters and events being described by the reciter, sometimes with, sometimes without the voice. The romantic and sentimental narrative poem by Tennyson goes well in German, and the work has great charm if a somewhat faded beauty. The other embellished recitation is based on a poem by Ludwig Uhland and called *Das Schloss am Meer* (The Castle by the Lake), Opus 45. Here the situation calls for question and answer. Again it is a tragic story, but cast in a different mould.

His chamber compositions occupy only six opus numbers. Of them the Wind Serenade for 13 instruments, Opus 7, is substantial in context rather than length. Its one movement lasts for about 10 minutes and contains some typically Straussian passages, especially when there are provokingly distant keys from which to modulate in time to bring the section back to its tonic. This is indeed one of Strauss's hallmarks. The Serenade is scored for double woodwind with contra-bassoon and four horns. Although he later dismissed the Serenade as being no more than a decent job by a music student, Strauss showed in it great feeling for the handling of wind instruments, in which his father aided and abetted him.

The Piano Quartet, opus 13, was given in Weimar in 1885 with the composer at the piano; it is a delightful work, partly because the first three movements are almost wholly based on the 'new' music of Brahms, which Strauss had fallen for, and was imitating. Thanks to Brahms, Strauss found a means whereby he was able to adhere closely to sonata form and to develop his ideas logically and without apparent effort.

Above: Strauss's workroom at Garmisch, which has been left with all effects and furniture in the same position as in his lifetime.

The sonata for Cello and Piano in F is an ambitious work, but structurally shows Strauss fumbling to arrive at the kind of security which he was soon to reach in the Piano Quartet. Yet this lack of felicity does not immediately strike one since the sonata's opening draws one along with a grand impetuosity which appealed to the great violinist Joachim when he heard its first performance. At an early age, Strauss had learnt that to create an impressive and gripping opening to a composition was the surest way of capturing the audience's attention from the first. Later he was to criticize Stravinsky's *Firebird* suite along the same lines lecturing the Russian sternly: 'Your *Firebird* begins too softly. You will never hold an audience's attention from the start like that. You should begin loudly; I find it very successful.'

The Violin Sonata is the last chamber work that Strauss wrote—though perhaps too heavily influenced by Schumann, it is a fine piece. He was working on it concurrently with the tone poems *Macbeth* and *Don Juan*, and it seems to have emerged so reluctantly that it is a wonder it was ever finished. It took a full year and bears an obviously close relationship to the Violin Concerto, which it followed.

There are only two conventional concertos

Opposite above: Richard Strauss with Heinz Tietjen (conductor, producer and intendant at the Berlin Opera) and the young conductor Herbert von Karajan, taken in 1942.

Opposite below: Strauss shown at his home in Garmisch, writing the full score of Die schweigsame Frau *from his notes.*

to have been published from this early period: the Violin Concerto in D minor, opus 8; and the first Horn Concerto in E♭, opus 11. Of the two, the concerto for horn is undoubtedly superior. Both are instructive in the way Strauss uses the solo instrument; he was playing the violin himself a good deal at the time he wrote the concerto for it, while his father's prowess on the horn made certain that every possibility was given to opus 11. Oddly enough, the horn concerto was not dedicated to Franz Strauss, but to Oscar Franz, a player and established teacher of the instrument. As it turned out, old Strauss found the solo part too taxing for him to dare to play in public, and (although it did receive an earlier performance with piano accompaniment) at its first orchestral hearing, delayed until two years after its completion, it was given by the Meiningen Orchestra under von Bülow and their first horn player Gustav Leinhos was the soloist. This

was in March 1885. The most striking thing about this ebullient and amazing work is in Strauss's use of the same thematic material for the concerto's opening and for its third movement, here changed into 6/8 time, a bold and advanced thought. The strong and elegant use of the solo instrument and the confident orchestration, together with a rejection of sonata form in the outer movements, all add up to making this by far the most important and interesting of these early works. The Violin Concerto of the previous year cannot match it. Although Strauss shows a natural affinity for and understanding of the violin, the work is pale and patchy, and by no means as effective as the horn concerto's sound.

Perhaps the point has now been reached when we can attempt to define the characteristics of Strauss's mature style. They are to be found in his melodies, his form and harmonies, and in his orchestration. The melodies are remarkable for the huge sweep of their phrases, like great arches which threaten to stay up at the keystone and hang suspended there before descending. One has only to remember the opening of the Trio in the last act of *Der Rosenkavalier*, or of any opening phrase to a work or to a movement, for that matter. This sweep gives the impression of great energy because of the compass of notes each phrase encloses. Such freedom of line again leads Strauss to great possibilities for luxurious harmonies. Strauss's technical mastery was complete and he could certainly have composed to the strictest academic forms but this was not his way. He did not squeeze himself into a preconceived musical shape, he made the shape fit his needs. At the time when they first appeared, most of Strauss's tone-poems were described as they sounded—'chaotic', in form and in harmony. Today they are perfectly intelligible though some of the remarkable harmonic colourations to be found for example in *Salome* and *Elektra* remain bold and invigorating. All this wealth, first of melodic curves, next of harmonic richness, thirdly of highly individual form leads, naturally, to lavish orchestrations. One can point to 'cut-down' versions of the tone-poems and the suites from the operas and say that they are perfectly adequate, but this begs the question, in fact beggars it. Strauss was for ever purposely trying to shock his listeners and managing to do so easily, just as avant-garde composers today are trying the same thing with the same means, although by different methods. For a composer to be 'modern' means that he has not only to be in step with the century and with its youth, but if possible to be ahead of them all so that he can prophesy what future audiences will enjoy. Whether today's composers will succeed it is too early to say; but Strauss did succeed at first although nobody in their right mind would have stated that Strauss was anything but a destroyer of everything that the accepted musical values stood for. He spoke to his contemporary audiences and disgusted them with what they heard; but what he said was nevertheless completely intelligible to their children in less than 50 years—even faintly out of date.

Strauss's gift for counterpoint is clearly discernible in most of his mature works. On many occasions one wants to be able to listen more deeply than to the melodic line, beautiful though it may be, in order to discern what may be going on underneath it—and there may be a number of other ideas all at once. Strauss never wasted a single bar on any stave, and although he may be accused of overloading his score page and of stifling the listener's listening capacity, he was never, until the late 1920s, uninventive. Even during the First World War, he was still writing for gargantuan orchestras because it was expected of him, and also because they were easily available. Germany was a huge, strong, tough and rich nation, demanding the kind of music which Strauss was able to match with his *Alpensinfonie* or his opera of 1918 *The Woman without a Shadow*.

On either side of this opera lie *Ariadne on Naxos* and *Intermezzo*—*Ariadne* with its 23-man band, and *Intermezzo* with its 50, most of which are reserved for interludes rather than for supporting the terse and economical sung-speech which never requires more than the minimum of players. When he had no other demands imposed upon him, Strauss seems to have been at home with smaller forces.

Harmonically and melodically one can scarcely do better than to reach for the score of *Der Rosenkavalier* to find the indelible stamp of nearly everything that Strauss had to say. It is a macrocosm of his output with its sweetness, delicacy and gentility offset by coarseness, garishness and boorishness. These stark contrasts in the music reflect the man. The earthy quality in Strauss as a good Bavarian

Caricature of Strauss by H. Lindoff (about 1918), which gives a clue to Strauss's own mischievous sense of humour.

citizen comes out all the time, while behind the glories of some of the most ecstatic moments there is the prompting that we are all human. Strauss's brand of humour was not of the somewhat heavy Bavarian kind but above all he was as sincere as he was mischievous.

The border-line between Strauss's symphonies and his tone-poems is sometimes a thin one. There are compositions which he called 'Symphony': No. 1 in D minor (1880 and unpublished), and No. 2 in F minor, opus 12 of 1884. They are both in four movements and are quite clearly what Strauss calls them. But *Aus Italien* comes near to being a symphony. This is a descriptive work culled from Strauss's impressions gained from his first visit to Italy in 1886. It may be said to be the stepping-stone between symphony and tone-poem. The first symphony was completed in only three months and Norman Del Mar says that it 'is very much the same vintage as the String Quartet, though on the whole rather less self-assured.' The second symphony has been recorded (once and indifferently) and it only makes one wonder at the huge strides which Strauss was to make between it and *Don Juan*, all in the space of five years. Yet von Bülow liked this symphony and played it at Strauss's Meiningen début, when Brahms was present. Brahms told Strauss 'Your Symphony is too full of thematic irrelevancies. There is no point in piling up themes which are only contrasted rhythmically on a single triad.' In saying this, Brahms was perfectly naturally comparing Strauss's symphony with his own four, but he was, after all, a slave to the rigid symphonic form, and was most likely unable to appreciate that the young composer was already ventilating his extraordinary talent for counterpoint.

Yet, the work is altogether uninteresting by comparison with those around it and those which came later, and it is not surprising that it is never played nowadays.

But *Aus Italien* is another matter. It was Brahms who had suggested that it would benefit Strauss more to take a holiday in the South after leaving Meiningen, than to fritter away his time in Berlin. Strauss took his advice and was entranced with what he found, and basking in the sunshine of Italy he was refreshed and inspired to work. Ever afterwards he found that he was far better able to work when the sun shone than when the weather was dull or wet. The ruins of the Roman Forum affected him most and he was inspired to compose a piece about it. Probably at this stage in his career, Strauss, although on the threshold of revitalizing the tone-poem, was not yet sufficiently confident to launch himself into this form or to organize into one movement all the material which would go so much more simply into four. So he called *Aus Italien* a 'symphonic fantasy'; it was dedicated to von Bülow. At its first performance in Munich in March 1887, which Strauss conducted, the work was greeted with such jeers and catcalls as to make Franz Strauss angry and even worried for his son's reputation. But the composer was delighted. He had shattered the reactionary clique in Munich and had clearly proclaimed himself a 'modern', especially by his uncon-

The first study in A major by Strauss of the Sonnet from Capriccio, *in Professor Hans Swarosky's hand. Strauss dedicated this song to Swarosky since he had been of immense help to Strauss and Clemens Krauss during the writing of the libretto for the opera.*

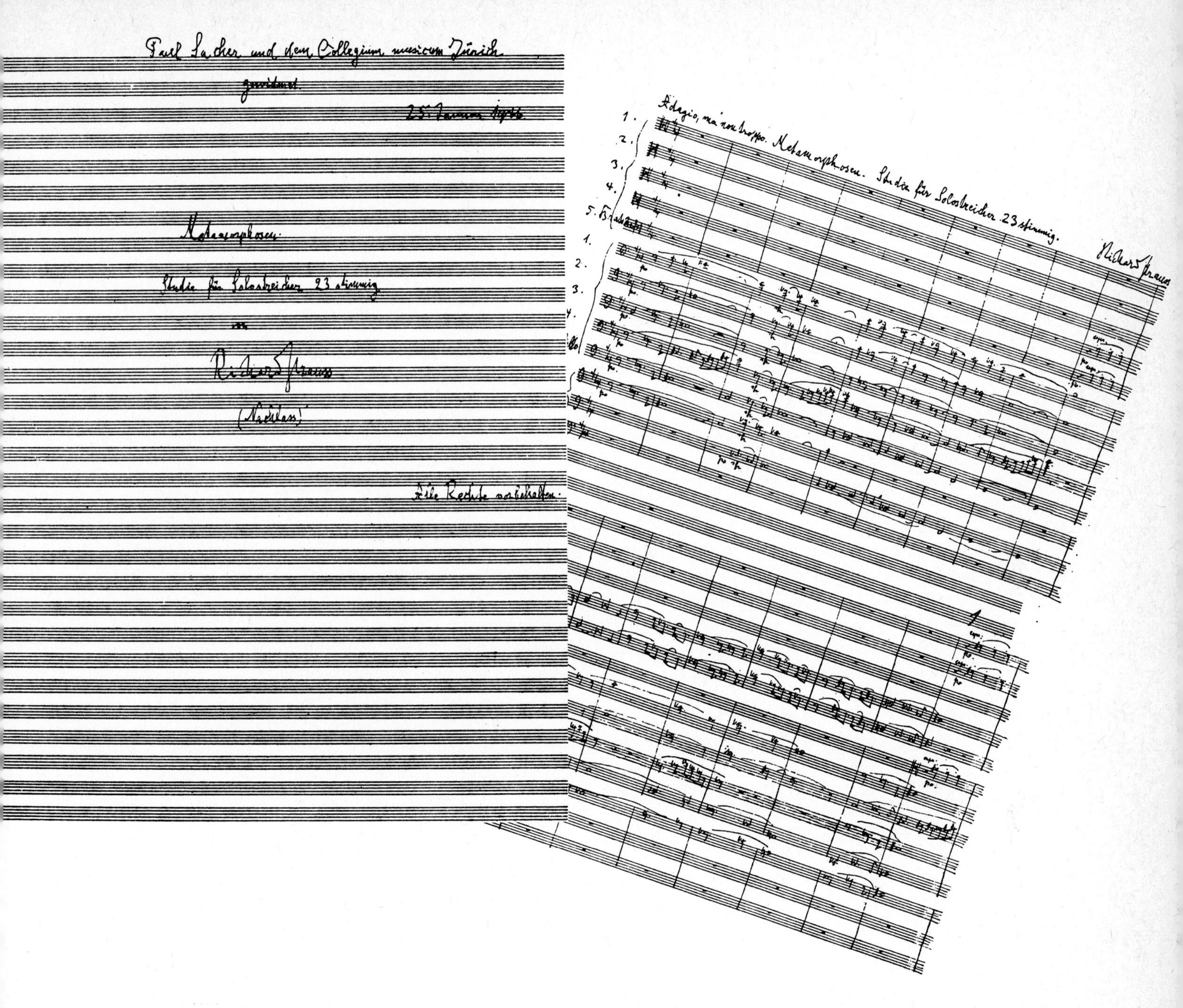

Title page and first page of the original manuscript score of Metamorphosen.
See page 105.

scious take-off, in the last movement, of Luigi Denza's popular song *Funiculi Funicula*. Levi, Ritter and Strauss's family all supported him, so it was with great pride that he wrote to his uncle: 'I now comfort myself with the knowledge that I am on the road I want to travel, fully conscious that there has never been an artist who was not considered mad by thousands of his fellow-men.'

Twenty-one songs and the Violin Sonata separate *Aus Italien* from the tone-poems (a term which Strauss preferred to 'Symphonic Poems') and when they arrived, three came together. The first one to be heard was *Don Juan*, and this marks the beginning of Strauss's immediate success as a composer. This Don Juan is not the same as Gluck's or Mozart's, but is the result of fragments of a verse-play by the mentally unstable Nicholas Lenau. It tells how Don Juan's father sends his other son to bring Juan back from his life of depravity. Juan himself, having exhausted the full range of erotic and emotional experience in his quest of the perfect woman, and having hurt or injured many others in his quest, becomes disgusted with the pattern of his life. He purposely allows his guard to drop during a duel, so as to feel yet another new experience—this time Death.

Strauss was fascinated by the psychological approach to the story and set about the business of interpreting it in music, wholeheartedly. He chose four episodes which emphasize the story, yet he did not attempt an exact musical equivalent of Lenau's verse. The massive first subject, which becomes part of a sonata first movement with insertions, is itself a germ-cell of themes which are separately developed later. So no wonder that it sounds strong, burstingly passionate and masculine! The love-theme is, by contrast, among one of Strauss's most gloriously feminine ideas, and the whole organization of the tone-poem, together with its rich colours and rapturous evocation of sunshine, lechery and—at the end—pathetic weariness of life, makes the whole work an immensely compelling experience. Erotic it most certainly is. Strauss was, for the first time, illustrating the more seamy side of life, while at the same time treating it as a perfectly normal thing to do, by expressing, as far as he was able, the whole of life and its people, even the more despicable and wicked. *Don Juan* was composed between 1887–89; next came another tone-poem, *Tod und Verklärung* '*Death and Transfiguration*' (opus 24) which was composed between 1888–89. It was performed only seven months after *Don Juan* and concerns the last painful thoughts of a dying man, an artist 'perhaps', Strauss adds. The character portrayed re-lives, in a few minutes, the whole of his past life and then the glories of the Hereafter are revealed to him as his soul flies upward, to the glory that his body was never able to reach. There is little doubt that there is an autobiographical element in this—as there is in all the tone-poems, though up to this time, Strauss had not been as desperately ill as he was soon to be. An aspect of this autobiographical nature lies in the fact that Strauss used the *Transfiguration* motif, albeit briefly, in both the Lied *Frühlingsfeier* (opus 56/5), as well as in one of his last songs, *Im Abendrot*.

The tone poem falls into two distinct parts: that which describes the dying man, with a brilliant re-creation of his sufferings, and that which far less successfully attempts to portray the celestial vision. It is the first of several attempts at representing the idea of Paradise or Heavenly Bliss and, like all the others, it fails to fulfill its high ambitions; perhaps Richard Strauss had his feet too firmly on the ground for such exalted and ethereal themes. The section in *Death and Transfiguration* is built on a seemingly monumental but hollow subject which is exploited beyond its resources while Strauss's puzzling choice of the key of C major almost ensured that his inspiration deserted him.

By comparison, *Till Eulenspiegel* is probably the most extrovert, the most endearing and the best-loved of all Strauss's tone-poems, wrapped, as it is, within a start and a finish that proclaims it all a fairy-tale. We can easily follow the mischievous little pixie-man through his infuriatingly good-natured antics which eventually go too far and bring him to the gallows. At one time Strauss considered writing a one-act opera about Till, but he never developed the idea and instead composed this work which he described as a classical Rondo. It all adds up to Strauss hugely enjoying humorous situations, and as much of the essence of the legendary Till crops up time and time again in Strauss's own sayings, there is one, simple and autobiographical conclusion to be drawn.

Macbeth and *Don Quixote* represent, in their different ways, Strauss's success in psychological representation of character through the orchestra, or programme music with a twist. *Macbeth* was the first tone-poem to be completed, in advance of *Don Juan*, but when von Bülow saw that the work ended with a triumphant march for Malcolm, he persuaded Strauss that this would not do when the title of the piece is something else. *Macbeth* remained unplayed in its first version save for one occasion when Strauss found himself able to run it through with the Mannheim Orchestra, entirely for his own benefit. Then he put it away and did not bring it out until after *Death and Transfiguration* had been given. In its revised form, with a certain fining down of the instrumentation and a new ending, Strauss approved it, but we seldom hear it today. It is said that Strauss was not at all keen on its inclusion in Beecham's festival at Drury Lane in 1947, for he had long since spoken with a very different voice. Interesting as it is, those works which followed it were vastly more impressive, especially *Don Quixote*.

Here is something that is classified as a tone-poem, but which is more often set out on the concert platform as if it were a cello concerto.

Strauss in Paris in 1930 with the director of the Théâtre des Champs Elysées—the scene of his Parisian opera premières and association with Romain Rolland.

The solo (or principal) cello more or less corresponds to the mentally shattered Don, while the principal viola, a far less taxing part, speaks for Sancho Panza most of the time. The form of the piece is completely original although its construction is based on a theme and set of ten variations, each one corresponding to an episode in the story of 'Don Quixote' as told by Cervantes, though not necessarily in his order. Not that this matters, for Strauss manages in a remarkable way to pin down the personality of the strange, half-demented dreamer, Don Quixote; and even though critics, past and present, have tended to focus their attention and strictures upon the musical portrayal of the bleating sheep and the windmills and the other unlikely objects in the vivid story, there is far more of real interest to be gained by studying the gradual disintegration and demise of the already crumbling mind, and its final, truly touching submission to death. *Don Quixote* is Strauss's opus 35 and was first performed in Cologne in March 1898.

If *Don Quixote* broke new ground, *Ein Heldenleben*, the last of the self-styled tone-poems, extended this form as far as was possible. Appropriately enough, Strauss conducted the first performance himself, and astounded as well as disgusted many in that first audience (and in subsequent ones) by the daring expedients to which he went in order to relate the antics of himself, his wife and the adversaries via the orchestra. In particular, the three squeaky flutes which come in from time to time and the episode of the parallel sevenths, which were for a long time considered to be outrageously unharmonic by any standards show how advanced were Strauss's compositional and orchestral techniques in these years immediately preceding the turn of the century. *A Hero's Life* still sounds very fresh, and constantly yields new finds even to those who have heard it frequently; but it has weathered most changing musical tastes and events and today it seems far more moving and perceptive than ugly and unappealing. The composition is in six sections, the whole cast in a symphonic mould, but with an extremely important part for solo virtuoso violin whose comments, reflections, characterizations and cadenzas often seem to weigh as much as if it were a concerto. It is a very powerful work. The battle sequence in particular is often so stirring as to catch one up in its power and make one wonder (having survived the battle and feeling like a real veteran) how Strauss, who was never a soldier, was able to penetrate the meaning of it all so accurately and then to have portrayed it in music. *A Hero's Life* calls for a huge orchestra: 64 strings, quadruple woodwind, 8 horns, 5 trumpets, 3 trombones and 2 tubas, a great deal of percussion and 2 harps, and was performed at Frankfurt in March 1899.

Strauss's fifth tone poem, *Also sprach Zarathustra* based 'freely' on Nietzsche, can scarcely be said to contain any of the anti-Christian or anti-human elements of that totalitarian poem. Its *second* (but not its first!) opening phrase has become internationally known by its use in a space film, subsequently as accompaniment to astronauts' activities on television, which is doubtful fame indeed. The work itself is of over half an hour's duration, somewhat rambling and unless one can identify passages from Nietzsche, from the point of view of its title, can be taken only as symphonic, not programme music.

The *Alpensinfonie* dates from 1915 and is a one-movement composition in 22 continuously played episodes which describe the ascent of a mountain within the framework of nature portrayed from night and sunrise, through mists which obscure the sun, a thunderstorm, and night once more after sunset. Strauss's orchestration for this work is more luxurious than ever, and quite astonishing considering that it was written during the First World War. However, it is interesting to find that on two former occasions Strauss considered writing a piece about the Alps, once when he was very young indeed and had been on holiday in the Tirol, and again between *Heldenleben* and the *Domestica*. And although the *Alpensinfonie* was first heard in 1915, Strauss had been at it, on and off, since 1911, so the subject obviously meant a lot to him. What he has left us is all too plainly from the beginning of his decline, when he was note-spinning with immense effort. There are countless reminiscences in the *Alpensinfonie*, but its huge framework and sound do not make up for a certain paucity of invention, a complete paucity of inspiration.

Altogether Strauss composed 213 songs; twelve of these have disappeared but are documented. He wrote 196 true Lieder, that is to say songs with piano accompaniment, but when orchestrated the works become more important and are no longer Lieder in the strictest sense. Twenty-six of his songs have both piano and orchestral versions, while a further seventeen composed for voice and orchestra have printed piano reductions for rehearsal purposes.

For the most part, Strauss took his words from popular contemporary German poets whose works are unknown outside Germany: poets such as Hermann von Gilm, A. F. von Schack, Felix Dahn, Karl Henckell, Otto Bierbaum and others. There are a few songs to poems by Goethe and Schiller, and three from *Hamlet*. Strauss set only two poems which Schubert had also used—*Das Rosenband* and *An Sie* by Klopstock—but in addition he used many poems which his own contemporaries were setting, generally unwittingly of each other, simply because they were in fashion.

A handful of Strauss's Lieder have become so well-known that a few need be mentioned by name: *Ruhe meine Seele*, *Cäcilie*, *Heimliche Aufforderung* and *Morgen!* all opus 27 and Strauss's wedding present to his wife; *Zueignung* and *Allerseelen* of opus 10; *Traum durch die Dämmerung* of opus 29; *Befreit* opus 39; *Wiegenlied* opus 41; and *Die Heiligen drei Könige* of 1906.

Perhaps Strauss's most significant and original contribution to German Song is to be found in his orchestrations. The most advanced of these are the so-called 'Four Last Songs', which are always sung as a set but in a different order from that in which they were composed and remained when he died. Of course we do not know whether he intended them to remain as four songs since he was in any case about to compose another song of which only a few bars are extant. In any case no other groups of his songs are ever sung together as printed except the *Krämerspiegel* set of 1918 and sometimes the opus 68 set, either with piano or, more rarely, with orchestra. Invariably Strauss's enhanced settings for orchestra merely amplify what the piano did in its own way, with instrumental felicities and greater, more luscious support to the voice. But in the case of *Ruhe meine Seele*, orchestrated in 1948 at the same time as he was writing the 'Four Last Songs', and at a time of great depression, Strauss radically changed its original mood of over half a century before, darkening it and making it far more pessimistic. The charming opus 68 is very nearly a song cycle. Strauss composed it for Elizabeth Schumann when she became the prime exponent of this side of his art, in succession to Frau Strauss whose voice had deteriorated. It is especially a woman's group of songs and it is strange that in his magnificent record album of 131 of Strauss's Lieder, Fischer-Dieskau should have chosen to sing two of them.

We have a few examples on gramophone records of Strauss accompanying singers in his own Lieder (Heinrich Schlusnus and Robert Hutt on 78's and Maria Reining, Lea Piltti and Anton Dermota from Austrian Radio tapes on a limited circulation LP). The LP shows one example of Strauss improvising an accompaniment which is quite fascinating. It is only a pity that no recording seems to exist of Strauss accompanying his wife.

In attempting to assess Strauss's worth and his importance as a Lieder composer, one must acknowledge his superb flow of melody; his acute understanding of a singer's needs in high vowel values; breathing; pointing of words, and the accompanying texture which allows the meaning of these words to be heard. Moreover, in the orchestrated songs he extends his great experience of the opera house to the concert hall, where the pellucid accompaniments offer a combination of great richness and clarity of support to the singer. In the latter years opera, which had taken Strauss away from Lieder composition for twelve years, amply paid back what it owed by way of the orchestral and orchestrated songs.

A prominent feature of German musical life at the turn of the century were the choral festivals held all over the country. Strauss was much sought after as an adjudicator. Competitions between male voice choirs were generally an important event at these festivals and Strauss became interested in this combination of voices and wrote a number of works for it; among them is his only setting of words by Hofmannsthal outside the field of opera. In addition he wrote a number of other choral works and various other compositions for voice. Even these miscellaneous compositions can occasionally open new insights to a better understanding of this versatile composer while the tone poems and Lieder discussed in this chapter occupy a major place in his creative output. However it is of course the operas that are generally acknowledged to be his greatest achievement and it is now time for us to look at these more closely.

Posed period portrait by E. O. Hoppe.

Chapter 5

Strauss and Opera-1

Strauss's achievement in opera may be divided into two clear, though temperamentally unequal parts. This achievement begins with the uncertainty of *Guntram*, and the freer style of *Feursnot*, uncomplicated by Wagnerian influences; and then it crashes into an altogether original and exciting region of psychological drama with *Salome* and *Elektra*. Then there comes another switch to the sweet bitterness of *Der Rosenkavalier*, Strauss's most successful opera in terms of popular esteem and financial reward, but also his operatic watershed. Every stagework which followed has been considered as either unintelligible, undistinguished or unacceptable except to the highly sophisticated (or pretentious) few. We shall try to find out whether this opinion is valid, in the next chapter, but first, let us explore the importance of the earlier operas.

We know how *Guntram* was rehearsed, and how bitter Strauss was over its failure to be appreciated either in Weimar or in Munich. He had put a great deal of time and effort into it and for a while he found it hard to accept that it had all been in vain. Strauss called his hero Guntram, not a real name at all, but one which, it can only be supposed, is a combination of the names of two Wagnerian characters: Gunther in *Götterdämmerung* and Wolfram in *Tannhäuser*. There is no connection between Strauss's Guntram and either hero. It merely shows how deeply influenced Strauss was by Wagner.

During the composition of both the poem and the score, Strauss told von Bülow all he was doing, and the elder man commented:

> I am much struck by your interesting information that you are thinking of a 'dramma lirico'. I have confidence in your young creative power and hope that you will achieve the necessary degree of artistic somnambulism. Take care of yourself, and accept the friendliest greetings from yours, Ever most faithfully H.v.Bülow. In haste and heat.

The tone of this letter makes it evident how close they were when von Bülow was not in one of his suspicious moods, and how valuable his advice was to Strauss at all times. But after a few months, von Bülow seemed less convinced that his protégé was on the right lines, and so he attempted to interest him instead in Ibsen's play *Banquet at Solhaug* which had only recently appeared in Germany in translation. It is a play about the love of two sisters for the same man, and consequently far too bourgeois for the kind of lofty subject which the young Strauss had in mind. He wrote his libretto for *Guntram*, undeterred by suggestions from many other friends besides von Bülow, and composed the opera abroad in Greece, Egypt, Sicily and Italy during a period of long convalescence. In all it took six years until its appearance on the Weimar stage where, he wrote, it had exactly the desired effect, and the one which he had anticipated. This was, of course, a highly satisfactory technical accomplishment. However, there were more cancellations of future planned productions elsewhere than there were performances of it. The one-performance revival in Munich a year after Weimar involved the cast and orchestra in a revolt against Strauss and put paid to a revival anywhere else, although it is remarkable that other, celebrated opera houses like Berlin, Dresden and Hamburg had been prepared to bill the work on Strauss's name alone.

The main reason for *Guntram*'s lack of appeal—far more now than then—lies in the outdated and poorly constructed libretto with its boring and priggish hero, determined to redeem people wherever he goes, and in spite of their inclinations. There are some astonishing examples of the later Strauss in the very long score, but also pages and pages of utter tedium. *Guntram* was revived as a special kind of present to Strauss in 1940 in Weimar, when he made substantial cuts which reduced the

Opposite: The 1969 Visconti production of Der Rosenkavalier *at the Royal Opera House Covent Garden, London, with sets by Scarfiotti; showing the presentation of the silver rose in Act 2 with Josephine Veasey as Octavian and Joan Carlyle as Sophie.*

Right: A rare picture of a scene from Act 1 of the première of Strauss's first opera Guntram *in Weimar, showing Herr Schwarz as the wicked Duke and Heinrich Zeller as Guntram.*

Opposite above: Scottish Opera production of Der Rosenkavalier *1972, with sets by John Stoddart; with Helga Dernesch as the Marschallin and Janet Baker as Octavian in the first scene of the opera.*

Below: The Marschallin's levée in Act 1 of the same production with Helga Dernesch sitting right, and the Tenor Singer played by Derek Blackwell.

vocal score from its original size of 230 pages, to a slim 147.

It can be said that *Guntram*'s failure temporarily sickened Strauss with writing for the theatre. He was always interested in the medium, and was tempted by such subjects as *Till Eulenspiegel* which, as we know, came to nothing in this direction but which he distilled into the marvellous tone-poem.

In the autumn of 1898 Strauss met an interesting and stimulating writer in Munich, called Ernst von Wolzogen, who was quick to see that he might be able to catch Strauss in exactly the right mood and so provide him with an ideal libretto for an opera. The moment came when Strauss was telling Wolzogen about the insults that he had received when working in Munich and how he had, more or less, been thrown out with *Guntram*. Wolzogen saw revenge as the keyword and explained his idea to Strauss. But it was the composer who discovered the vehicle for their work, a Dutch legend which seemed exactly to fill the bill.

It tells how a burgomaster's daughter (Diemut) entices a new arrival in town (Kunrad) to her room one night. It is arranged that she will pull him up to the window of her room in a basket on a rope, but when he is half way up, she stops pulling, leaves him dangling in space, and then rouses the townspeople who gather round to jeer at him. Kunrad, however, is an apprentice magician, and calls on his master for support. The magician puts out every light in the town and through Kunrad tells people that the lights will come on again if Diemut yields to him, and of course she is obliged to do so. Wolzogen points to the association between the old magician (Wagner) and his apprentice (Strauss) by means of vile German puns within 'a linguistic style of rough, if somewhat archaic, joviality and with a decided tinge of dialect.' The libretto appealed enormously to Strauss who relished the opportunity to heap musical puns atop Wolzogen's literary ones. Naturally the opera was set in Munich, not the Netherlands, and Strauss decided to adapt his musical style accordingly. Wolzogen delivered the complete libretto in October 1900, and Strauss completed the full score with a dedication to Wagner on, appropriately enough, his birthday, 22 May 1901. The new opera is called *Feuersnot* ('Fire-famine') with the added connotation that *Feuer* can also mean sexual ardour—in which Diemut was apparently lacking until the lights went out.

A decade later, when Sir Thomas Beecham presented *Feuersnot* in London in a brilliantly witty English translation, he summed it up with the view: 'The chief feature of this gay

and audacious work are the number and difficulty of the choruses and the indelicacy of the story.' Strauss uses the waltz in this twelfth century story, and this fact was fastened upon by literally minded critics who preferred to notice and complain of this anachronism rather than concentrate upon the brilliant and original strokes and the well worked-out contrapuntal choruses. In fact, as Strauss employs it here, the waltz is not to be considered as a ballroom dance but as a means to set an atmosphere of ease and gaiety. Aided and abetted by the cabaret style of Wolzogen's text, Strauss often allows himself to sink into vulgarities in *Feuersnot*, which are only forgivable in the context of the story and its original purpose; but these same vulgarities of style were later to be polished up and deliberately re-presented in the character of Baron Ochs in *Der Rosenkavalier*.

If *Feuersnot* is not a masterpiece (indeed Strauss described it as a 'non-opera'), it marked the beginning of a new association with a theatre management with whom he kept faith, on and off, for 34 years. This was the Dresden State Opera, where nine of his premières took

K. K. Hof-Operntheater.

Mittwoch den 29. Jänner 1902

28. Vorstellung im Jahres-Abonnement.

Zum erstenmale:

Feuersnot.

Ein Singgedicht in einem Akt von Ernst v. Wolzogen. Musik von **Richard Strauß.**

Schweiker von Gundelfingen, Burgvogt . . . Hr. Breuer.
Ortolf Sentlinger, der Bürgermeister . . . Hr. Grengg.
Diemut, seine Tochter . . . Frl. Michalek.
Elsbeth, Wigelis, Margret, deren Gespielinnen . . . Frl. Kittel. Frl. v. Thann. Fr. Elizza.
Kunrad, der Ebner . . . Hr. Demuth.
Jörg Pöschel, der Leitgeb . . . Hr. Frauscher.
Hämerlein, der Fragner . . . Hr. Stehmann.
Kofel, der Schmied . . . Hr. Felix.
Kunz Gilgenstock, der Bäck und Bräuer . . . Hr. Marian.
Ortlieb Tulbeck, der Schäfflermeister . . . Hr. Schittenhelm.
Ursula, seine Frau . . . Fr. Kaulich.
Ruger Aspeck, der Hafner . . . Hr. Paul.
Walpurg, seine Frau . . . Frl. Kusmitsch.
Bürger, Bürgerinnen, Kinder, herzogliche Knechte.

Die Handlung spielt in München am Sonnwendtage, in alter Zeit „Subend" genannt, zu fabelhafter Unzeit.

Rouge et noir.

Ballet in 1 Vorspiel u. 3 Bildern von H. Regel. Musik von J. Bayer. Der choreographische Theil v. J. Haßreiter. 1. Bild. **„Die Blumenkönigin".** 2. Bild. **„Goldzauber".** 3. Bild. **„Der Ball nach Mitternacht".**

Witwe Hansen . . . Frl. Ellend.
Otto, Olga, ihre Enkel . . . Hr. Godlewski. Frl. Berger L.
Ein Dämon, Pelargie, Blumenmädchen . . . Frl. Krauß.
Fortuna . . . Frl. Sironi.
Die Elfenbeinkugel . . . Hr. Bradac.
Camillo de Saint-Gärce . . . Hr. Rathner F.
Der „Veilchenbaron" . . . Hr. Rathner Alf.
Vicomte de Chateau-Champ . . . Frl. Graselli.
Fiffi . . . Frl. Schimanek.
Florette
Ein Oberst a. D. der Republik San Marino . . . Hr. Zulka.
Dahomey, Congo-Fürst . . . Hr. Schreitter.
von Prittwitz auf Sprottenhausen . . . Hr. Kopetzki.
Amadeo, Lancieri-Lieutenant . . . Hr. Raimund.
Friedrich August Bliemchen, ein Sachse . . . Hr. Rathner Alf.
Elsa, seine Frau . . . Frl. Schreitter
Frau Kunze, Bliemchens Schwiegermutter . . . Frl. Graselli.
Beppo, ligurischer Schiffer, Pelargies Geliebter . . . Hr. Zulka.
„Dämon Gold" . . . Hr. Rumpel.
Mitglieder des „Pigeon Shooting-Club" (Taubenjägerinnen). Blumenmädchen. Curgäste. Ballgäste. Spieler. Croupiers. Diener.

Die Handlung des Vorspieles ereignet sich bei Wien; des 1. Bildes in Nizza; des 2. u. 3. Bildes in Monte Carlo.
Zeit: Die Gegenwart.

Vorkommende Tänze: 1. **Die Taubenjägerinnen:** Die Damen vom Corps de Ballet. — 2. **Bataille de fleurs:** Die Frls. Kohler, Konnert, Pellar, Wopalenski, Peterka, Gerzhofer, die Koryphäen und das Balletcorps. — 3. **Roulette:** Fortuna: Frl. Krauß. Die Elfenbeinkugel: Frl. Sironi, Herr Godlewski, die Damen vom Corps de Ballet und die Elevinnen. — 4. **„Gold und Silber."** Pas de deux: Frl. Sironi u. Hr. Guerra. — 5. **„Tarok-Polka":** Frl. Erich, Kohler, Wopalenski und Hr. van Hamme. — 6. **Karten-Ballabile:** Frl. Erich, Kohler, Wopalenski, Konnert, Pellar, Gerzhofer, Peterka, Seel, Weigang, Schreitter, Berger O., Hr. van Hamme und das Balletcorps.

Kostüme nach Zeichnungen von Franz Gaul. — Die neuen Dekorationen und die Vision im 2. Bilde nach R. Hennebergs Gemälde „Die Jagd nach dem Glück" von Brioschi jun. — Die Maschinerien und Beleuchtung vom Bühnen-Inspektor Herrn Julius Rudolph.

Der freie Eintritt ist heute ohne Ausnahme aufgehoben.

Der Beginn der Vorstellung sowie jedes Aktes wird durch ein Glockenzeichen bekanntgegeben.

Abendkassen-Eröffnung gegen halb 7 Uhr Anfang 7 Uhr. Ende gegen 10 Uhr.

Donnerstag den 30. Hoffmann's Erzählungen.
Freitag den 31. Excelsior. (Anfang **halb 8** Uhr.)
Samstag den 1. Februar. Mignon.
Sonntag den 2. Die Meistersinger von Nürnberg. (Anfang **halb 7** Uhr.)
Montag den 3. Hoffmann's Erzählungen.
Dienstag den 4. Feuersnot. — Hierauf: Rouge et noir.

Zum Dienstgebrauche.

Above: Semper's Opera House in Dresden, totally destroyed in 1945, scene of premières of nine of Strauss's operas.

Opposite above: Set design for an early production of Feuersnot *in 1902, based on true-to-life buildings in Munich.*

Opposite below: Playbill for the première of Feuersnot *in Dresden in 1902.*

place between 1901 and 1935. The Director of this beautiful old house was Ernst von Schuch, an adventurous and enterprising impresario, who was perfectly prepared to take risks in an atmosphere where the arts were generally encouraged, enjoyed and well supported. The Berlin Opera refused to take *Feuersnot* on moral grounds, despite Strauss's connection as Court Conductor. He promptly wrote to the administrative director

> I take the liberty of . . . informing you with respectful thanks, that I hereby renounce once and for all both the honour of having *Feuersnot* performed for the first time at the Berlin Opera House, and also the distinction of seeing any of my other dramatic works presented there.

He stood by this, and Berlin never had a Strauss world première. His letter came as such an insult to the management that the prim and bigoted Empress, who soon got to hear about it, endeavoured (without success) to have Strauss removed. But Berlin could afford to wait for its own revenge, and when it came, one feels that the file which had been accumulating until 1935 had possibly been opened in 1900.

When ruminating on *Feuersnot* at the end of his life, Strauss described it as an imperfect work, yet one that introduced a new style at the very beginning of a new century. And most aptly he called the work 'in its way a sort of upbeat'. The downbeat of his operatic career achieved a resounding crash with his next work, *Salome*.

Oscar Wilde was very fashionable in Western Europe at the turn of the century, and several composers saw the possibilities of turning his dramatic poem *Salomé* written in French, into an opera. Frederick Delius, the German born, English educated, French resident seized on it simultaneously with Strauss and so did a French composer called Mariotte. But it was Strauss who secured the rights to set Wilde's exotic poem. He went to Reinhardt's Deutsches Theater in Berlin and saw the Wilde play. On the way out he met a friend who asked him why he didn't write an opera on the work. Strauss replied: 'I've already started to do so!' He adapted the German translation by Hedwig Lachmann to his needs, tightening up the already terse story in one or two places to achieve even greater fusion of thought. By this act, Strauss altered the whole course of opera libretti, for this was the first deeply psychological German opera. The ugly characters of Herod and Herodias and the ambivalent personality of Salome herself are given such freedom of interpretation by Wilde, that Strauss had no difficulty at all in revealing these characteristics in an even more provocative fashion in his score. Salome's character can be interpreted more or less as one wishes and has been argued over incessantly. Substantiated by the score she appears either as a nymphomaniac, a mad adolescent, a normal adolescent driven mad at the end, or as a pure virgin who has always had her own way (because she is a princess) and sees no wrong in what she does, even when it comes to making love to the severed head of John the Baptist.

Strauss found himself up against two big difficulties. One lay in his treatment of the operatically uninteresting character of the Baptist (called Jokanaan), to whom he gave a lot of C major and some ungrateful and uncertain music to sing. The other difficulty was the hand of the censor in Berlin, Vienna and London which—after the successful Dresden première—lay heavily upon the biblical names of characters in the opera and many of the lines which they were required to utter. In Berlin it was allowed to take place providing that Salome prayed for redemption during her long, final soliloquy to the severed head, and that the Star of Bethlehem shone in the sky at the end as a token of optimism. Even granted these absurdities, the Emperor declared, with a shake of the head, that he was unhappy about the whole work, and he was certain it would do Strauss nothing but harm. In fact it paid for the construction of his villa in Garmisch!

Gustav Mahler who then ruled as conductor at the Vienna Opera, was so impatient to produce *Salome* there that he raced to try and beat the authorized Dresden première, with no less than four sopranos ready to sing the name-part, and with probably a finer cast than the one which the Saxon house had been able to muster. But the censor, supported by the city's Archbishop who possessed the most appropriate name of Piffl, prevented the Viennese performance altogether. *Salome* was not staged in Vienna until 1918.

In London in 1910, Sir Thomas Beecham followed his successful production of *Elektra* when he presented *Salome* at Covent Garden. In his memoirs, he tells how he was able to get it past the censor only by spending the weekend with the prime minister, Asquith, and then promising that the singers would learn their parts again in a bowdlerized version of the original German. He writes: 'Gradually I sensed by that telepathy that exists between the conductor of the orchestra and the artists on the stage, a growing restlessness and excitement of which the first exhibition was a slip on the part of Salome, who forgot two or three sentences of the bowdlerized version and lapsed into the viciousness of the lawful text.' As the opera continued, things got completely out of hand until all the singers had restored the original text as if the other had never existed. Beecham continues: 'I was powerless to intervene, and visions of disaster crowded upon my agitated brain. . . . After what seemed an age of purgatory to me, the performance came to an end, the public was enthusiastic, and the artists overflowed with delight at their success . . . While I remained on the stage with them after the curtain had gone down I was horrified to see advancing towards me the party from the Lord Chamberlain's box . . . To my delight the magnate addressed me with beaming countenance: "It has been wonderful; we are all delighted, and I felt I could not leave the theatre without thanking you and your colleagues for the complete way in which you have met and gratified our wishes." ' Beecham never knew whether the censor had been unable to understand the singers' words, or the German language, or whether he had been extraordinarily diplomatic under the circumstances.

At the Metropolitan Opera, New York, *Salome* survived only one performance because of petticoat authority in the city, and was not heard there again until 1933. Censors elsewhere also forbade the use of biblical names, or the presentation of a recognizable head on the charger. It appeared, variously as a blancmanage, a covered meat dish that was never opened, or as a shapeless mass beneath a piece of butter muslin, each of these, visual euphemisms being to any but the dullest imagination more objectionable than the 'real' thing.

All in all Strauss achieved a wild success with his 'scandalous' opera. It was not intended as cheap sensationalism nor was it scandalous for its own sake though the composer naturally had an eye to the eventual consequences when he

Opposite above left: Drawing by W. Bithorn portraying the excitement caused by Strauss's opera when it was first produced.

Above right: Mr Thomas Beecham in 1910, conductor of the first performance of Salome *in England at the Royal Opera House, Covent Garden in the same year.*

Below left: Eva von der Osten as Salome in the Dresden production. Eva von der Osten was the original Octavian in Der Rosenkavalier. *She was leading soprano at Dresden between 1902–30, but by then her voice was ruined. She collaborated in the first production of* Arabella *and was a faithful Strauss singer.*

Below right: A typical and informative London illustrated magazine impression of the first production of Salome *at Covent Garden. It not only shows details of the set but the mechanics of how Jokanaan arrived on the stage from the cistern. In the cameo (top left) there is a somewhat soulful portrait of Helga von Rappe who took over some performances from the London creator, Anino Ackte.*

Below: Ernst von Schuch. Director and conductor of the Dresden Opera who was responsible for the premieres of six of Strauss's operas there.

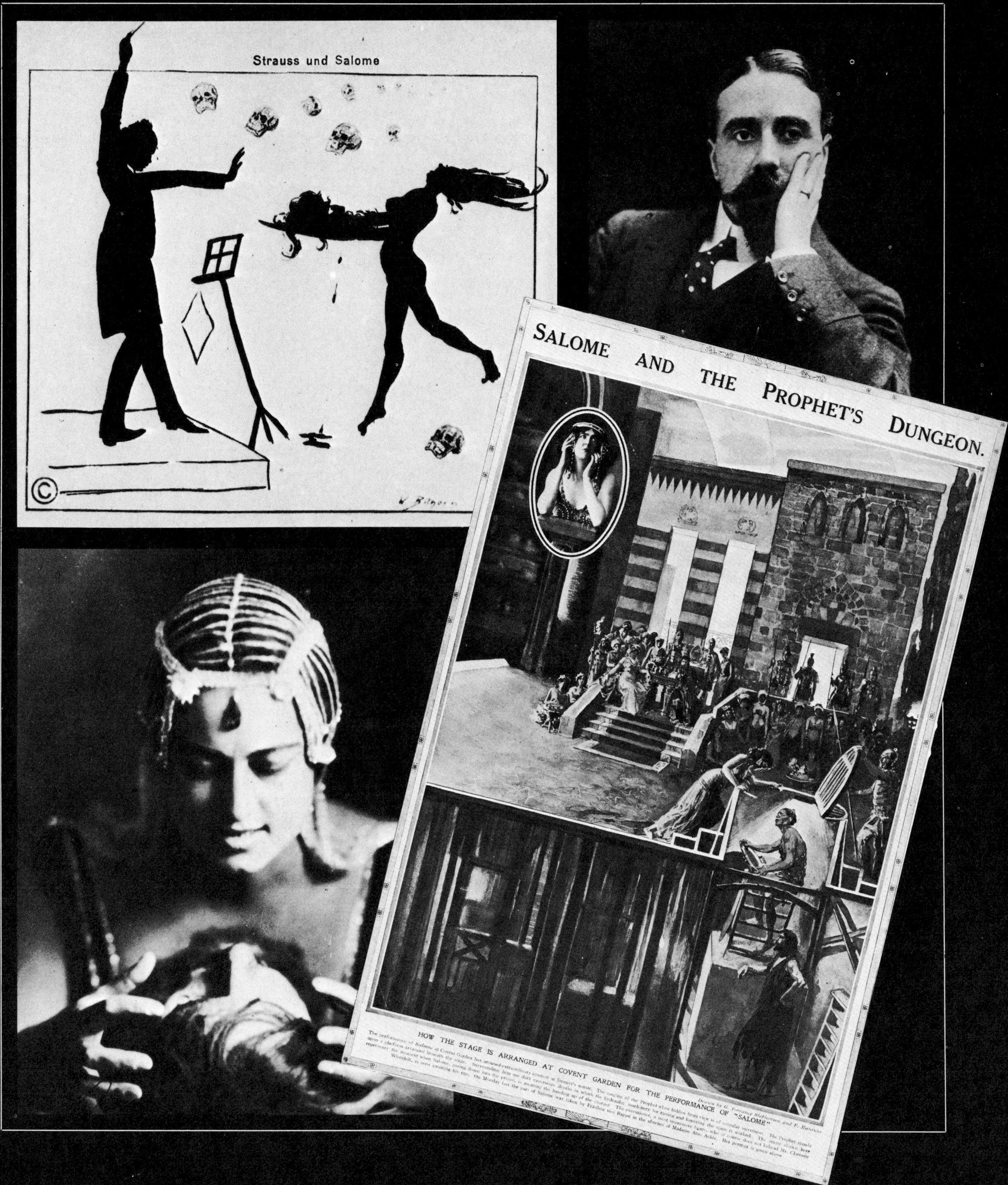

SALOME AND THE PROPHET'S DUNGEON.

Drawn by G. Torrance Stephenson and F. Matania

HOW THE STAGE IS ARRANGED AT COVENT GARDEN FOR THE PERFORMANCE OF "SALOME"

The performance of *Salome* at Covent Garden has aroused extraordinary interest in Strauss's music. The singing of the Prophet when hidden from view is of singular sweetness. The Prophet stands upon a platform arranged beneath the stage. Surrounding him are dark cavernous depths in which the hydraulic machinery for raising and lowering the stage is worked. The scene shown here represents the moment when Salome, gazing down into the prison, is awaiting the handing up of the charger. The executioner, a most impressive figure, who of course does not behead Mr. Clarence Whitehill, is seen awaiting his cue. On Monday last the part of Salome was taken by Fräulein von Rappé in the absence of Madame Aino Ackté. Her portrait is given above.

A vivid cartoon by Dolbin showing Strauss and Hofmannsthal in a coffee house in Vienna in the early twenties. The large gentleman behind Strauss is Richard Beer-Hofmann who is talking to Arthur Schnitzler

Opposite below: Set design by Salvador Dali for the 1949 production of Salome *at Covent Garden in Peter Brooke's production. The style and effect caused immense uproar in musical circles and led to the sets being destroyed after the eight performances that autumn.*
Opposite above: Ljuba Welitsch as Salome, with the 'head' of John the Baptist, and in another study. Because Dali did not arrive in London to supervise his part in the production, there were many inconsistencies and trivalities that might have been avoided; but the production was also disappointing because of an obvious decline in Madame Welitsch's singing powers since her last appearance in London in London 1947. The production might be summed up as a daring artistic effort that was badly handled, but was ten years in advance of its time.

was working on it. But in doing so he did not merely toss off a cheap work. Its strength comes from its very centre, and it contains some extremely advanced, brilliant and amazingly inventive musical strokes. The very start is gripping. The curtain goes up in silence, and immediately a solo clarinet runs up the scale as the singers on the stage come to life, and we recognize the terrace outside Herod's palace, bathed in moonlight. There are themes which signify moods as well as characters, and also events in their memories and their minds, which later on get woven into the texture of the opera as it becomes denser and fuller of reminiscences. The moon itself, with its mystical and physical association with woman, is ever present, though sometimes clouded; while by contrast Strauss draws with the utmost clarity and perception the debauched and disgusting figures of Herodias and her second husband, the lecherous Herod. Their music is unsavoury, while Salome's is pure and—at the start—even angelic. Eventually, when she has got her wish granted by her step-father and has Jokanaan beheaded there is one of the most exciting moments in all opera when we are waiting for the actual execution. Strauss calls upon four double basses to pinch their upper strings while bowing them, to create a particularly unhealthy and unearthly sound, representing a woman groaning. It achieves the most extraordinary effect. The nastiness of the whole comes across very forcibly and, as Strauss intended, we leave the theatre with an unpleasant taste in the mouth, only glad that Herod had the strength of purpose, after all, to have the awful child put to death by his soldiers. All through the opera there are contradictions, psychological, musical and visual, and the tenseness of the opening is seldom allowed to slacken. Even in an age of unabashed sensuality, *Salome* is a powerful piece, and Strauss's part in transforming a nasty poetic drama into a cruel and perverted opera, where his music underlines every wicked move and thought as with a blood-red line, can command nothing but our admiration, even if we find it rather strong medicine.

Strauss found Jokanaan's characterization beyond his grasp, and he also left Salome's Dance uncomposed until he had finished the rest of the opera. He came back afterwards and filled in the gap—and it sounds like it. The Dance is more frequently played as a concert piece than the opera is performed as a whole, yet it does not rise to anything like the creative impulse which enfolds it on either side. Furthermore it contains the waltz, and this makes a somewhat strange impression unless one accepts it in the way that has already been discussed with regard to *Feuersnot*.

In July 1905 Strauss first wrote to Romain Rolland about *Salome* in which he said 'Oscar Wilde originally wrote "Salomé" in French, and it is his original text which I want to use for my composition in its French adaptation . . . When I have finished it, who will be able to check that I haven't done violence to the French language?' It was as well that Strauss appealed to Rolland, for he had little if any idea of poetic French. Rolland realised this when he wrote 'The mute *e* is one of the great difficulties of the French language. One must really be careful not to eliminate it: it is one of the principal charms of our poetry; but it is very rare for a foreigner to have a real feeling for it. It's not so much a sound as a resonance, and an echo of the preceding syllable, which vibrates, hovers, and gently dies away in the air.' It may be imagined that this imaginative account was exactly what would appeal to Strauss, and for four months they were both at work on the text.

With *Salome*, Strauss emerged as one of the most interesting composers in Europe in the early years of the century. For in this work he had extended operatic form in a way that nobody had been able to do since the time of

Wagner, yet in a way that could not possibly have been predicted, even from the new directions hinted at in Wagner's *Parsifal*. All in all, *Salome* gives Strauss a place of first importance in the history of Western music.

After a successful run of the opera in Berlin, Max Reinhardt followed it with a new version of Sophocles' *Elektra*, written by the Austrian poet and man of letters, Hugo von Hofmannsthal. Strauss went to see this play and was tempted to consider it for operatic treatment as well, but his immediate desire was to find a more contrasting libretto. Hofmannsthal had tried in 1900 to tempt Strauss with an original book for a ballet but the already established composer had given him a total if charming brush-off. Now things had changed.

There is no better account to be found of the collaboration of a composer and librettist than in the published correspondence between Richard Strauss and Hugo von Hofmannsthal. It clearly traces the ways in which they initiated, discussed, shaped and achieved their intentions for more than 20 years. Indeed, as one reads it one becomes caught up with them both, like another member of the team. There is a rich fund of information and wisdom to be gained from these letters, which reveal much of the characters of the two men, and one can only marvel at the way in which they complemented each other, even though there were times of disagreement and discord, despite the often endearing tone of their address.

Hofmannsthal had rewritten and brought his version of *Electra* (in German, *Elektra*) up to date. The workshop correspondence starts here, on 7 March 1906, when the idea of the opera is taking shape. Strauss confesses to having doubts about a subject so similar to the one he is finishing (*Salome*) and mentions three other subjects which would greatly appeal to him: Semiramis and 'A really wild Cesare Borgia or Savonarola'. He did not realize how repugnant these suggestions were to Hugo von Hofmannsthal.

Hofmannsthal was born in Vienna in 1874, of mixed Austrian, Italian and Jewish descent. He was highly sensitive and would have been much more at home in the Renaissance, so fine was his intellect and so delicate his perception, than in the Europe of the late nineteenth century. The beautiful house at Rodaun, outside Vienna, in which he lived for most of his life, never belonged to him for the owner would not sell, and this irked him. Hofmannsthal was a considerable poet and writer quite apart from his association with Strauss. He had read the literary masterpieces of five European nations in the original languages by the time he was 30 and had a superb intellect. This was ceaseless in its probing and analyzing of a number of characters of his own invention which he kept in his mind until he had every single aspect of them worked out to his satisfaction. Sometimes this took years, and when the moment came for him to declare the character perfectly formed, he said it was 'safe'. Other characters affected him so much that he became ill with deep concern over the situations into which he had put them. One in particular, the hero of his play *The Tower*, could have no solution to his own problem, and the play was completed in several ways, but could, in fact, never be ended. This caused Hofmannsthal a tremendous amount of mental agony.

One may feel tempted to dismiss this brilliant poet as too brilliant, as a hopeless eccentric, so isolated and removed from real life as to torture himself with images which never lived. Could such a man enjoy and participate in life enough to be able to breathe real life into the characters he created? The answer is most certainly yes. We shall find out that the people who inhabit Hofmannsthal's libretti are every inch real, living men and women, one or two even a shade larger than life.

By comparison, Strauss may appear a trifle coarse, certainly less sophisticated, with his Bavarian accent (that he emphasized strongly when he wanted to create an effect) his ungainly, un-aristocratic appearance and his broad view of life. But this was not all there was to Strauss by any means, otherwise Hofmannsthal would never have worked with him. For Strauss too was very well read. He knew not only the German poets: Goethe, Schiller and a hundred others, but the Italians as well. His knowledge of Greek and Italian art was wide, and he spent as much of his spare time as he was able in Italy, and sometimes in Greece. He called himself a 'German Greek' from the first moment when he set eyes on that country.

As was only to be expected, two men of such talent did not always see eye to eye, but they generally came to an arrangement when artistic conflicts seriously affected one or the other of them. In fact Hofmannsthal was the one who was less willing to give in; Hofmannsthal was

Above: Anna Bahr-Mildenburg, the first Berlin and London Klytemnestra in Elektra. *She was married to the Austrian author, playwright, critic and theatre manager, Hermann Bahr, and lived in Salzburg.*

Right: Grace Bumbry as Salome *in the Covent Garden production by August Everding in 1970, with powerful sets and costumes by Andrzej Majewski.* *See also overleaf.*

Opposite: Die Frau ohne Schatten *at the Metropolitan Opera in New York in 1966, with production by Nathaniel Merril and sets by Robert O'Hearn. Top left: The first scene of the opera showing the Spirit Messenger (William Dooley) and the Nurse (Irene Dalis). Below: The transformation scene in Act I which shows the avaricious Dyer's wife (Christa Ludwig) being convinced that her hovel has been turned into a palace full of servants and riches.*

the angry one of the pair; Hofmannsthal was the one who had to be subdued and pacified with honeyed words, even though he had said hurtful and damaging things to and about the composer. But in the main it worked, and Hofmannsthal was by far the most important figure in Strauss's professional life. After a sensational start with *Elektra* and *Der Rosenkavalier*, Strauss and Hofmannsthal found themselves up against difficulties which they were unable to resolve, even in harness.

Hofmannsthal's libretto of *Elektra*, which he prepared for Strauss from his play, has a beautiful symmetry. The last section but one contains the psychological climax, and the final section holds the dramatic climax, and each section of the opera is fairly clearly defined:

1 Prologue, the Servants
2 Elektra
3 Elektra and Chrysothemis (i)
4 Elektra and Klytemnestra

after which point Strauss seems to emphasize the half-way mark by renumbering his rehearsal figures in the score 1a, 2a, 3a etc.

5 Elektra and Chrysothemis (ii)
6 Elektra and Orestes
7 Finale, the murders of Klytemnestra and Aegisthus, Elektra's Dance of Triumph and Death

There are certain initial points of similarity between *Elektra* and its predecessor *Salome*: the character of a demented woman in the name-part; a despicable step-father in Herod/Aegisthus; a horrible mother in Herodias/Klytemnestra; and a yearning, for sexual awakening on the part of Salome, and for revenge by Elektra. It is this last motive which distinguishes the two operas most completely. It is the driving force in Elektra's case, and after it has been accomplished, she has nothing to live for. In imagining that her brother was dead, she had taken on herself the responsibility for avenging her father Agamemnon's death by Aegisthus and Klytemnestra after his return from the Trojan Wars. It is only this which keeps her alive.

But although he is dead, the ghost of Agamemnon broods invisibly over the action, from the first utterance of the orchestra with a rhythmic figure which seems to speak his name: Ag—a—*mem*—non, a phrase which keeps on recurring. (Later Strauss was to use the same device in his opera *The Woman without a Shadow* to signal the brooding presence of the invisible god Keikobad.) Up to the moment when the distraught and defiled princess Elektra realizes that a tall stranger is none other than her brother Orestes, seemingly come back to life, she is to be the pivot of the action and the ritual act; but when Orestes has killed his mother and his step-father in revenge for their father's death, Elektra dies released of tension and of the need to live.

The most fascinating character in the opera is probably not Elektra at all, but Klytemnestra. As opposed to her rebellious daughter who is keeping herself alive by her will alone, Klytemnestra is slowly dying, not only of the physical diseases which have wracked her body, but also of mental agonies that keep her awake all night, terrified to sleep on account of the dreams which are even worse than her waking dreads. It is characteristic of both Hofmannsthal and Strauss that they settled on dreams, in the course of dialogue in the opera, and Strauss has painted a fearful accompaniment to illustrate Klytemnestra's tortured thoughts. Whereas in *Salome* he had purposely made much of his fine gift for counterpoint, and had composed passages in more than one key to be heard simultaneously, he pushes this even further in *Elektra* to what has been described as 'the very bounds of tonality'.

In other words, for perfectly logical reasons dictated by the characters in this opera, and by events in the course of its story, Strauss frequently sets passages in remote keys which are played together and result in the most extraordinary clashes and tensions. This is particularly striking in that masterpiece of thought and musical construction, Klytemnestra's Dream. Against these remarkable innovations there are equally beautiful moments when the action calls for them, such as the theme which relates to the once happy association of Elektra, Chrysothemis and Orestes when Agamemnon was their father and they were children; and the whole of the Recognition Scene between Elektra and Orestes, the nearest we ever get in this opera of hate to anything like to a mood of love and affection.

Everybody of artistic and social importance in Europe, so it has been said, was in the audience at the first performance of *Elektra* in Dresden on 25 January 1909. One can only reflect that this was either an overstatement or else the commentator's standards must have been remarkably high. Even so it emphasises the importance of Strauss's new opera that it should have attracted such attention. There is also some doubt as to the actual achievement of the first production: Hofmannsthal had a great many reservations about the way in which the joint ambition of poet and composer was carried out, but Strauss described it as 'one of the most beautiful and pure artistic experiences of my whole life'. He was in fact technically unable to conduct *Elektra* at first, and after an abortive few moments on the rostrum during a rehearsal, he handed the baton back to Ernst von Schuch who overcame all the fearsome difficulties which Strauss had composed for the orchestra and the singers.

Sir Thomas Beecham presented *Elektra* at Covent Garden in his 1910 season, during which Strauss—who by that time had mastered his own score—came over and conducted two performances of it. In 1947 Beecham again conducted two performances of *Elektra*, in the presence of the aged Strauss. Again there were conflicts as to the artistic worth of this performance, but the Recognition Scene and Finale were commercially recorded at the time. Today one can get privately issued tapes and records of the whole performance.

When we hear the work today in the opera house or on record, *Elektra* does not seem so outrageous, but its power is undeniable, and given a good performance on the stage it can be moving in the extreme. In setting this classical story Strauss not only bowed to his love of Greek legend, but used the full resources of the theatre to dig deep into the roots of human motivation and to touch those uncomfortable, hidden secrets which we all pretend are not there: our relationship with our parents, or conversely as parents with our own children. It has been stated that Strauss realized that he had gone as far as he could and was afterwards anxious to set an operetta-like work for a change; but this is not easy to believe when we see from the correspondence with Hofmannsthal how he constantly asks for heavily dramatic libretti.

In summing up Strauss's operatic achievements so far, we must remember that he was not yet 45, was at the peak of his creative career, he had a large following, huge prestige and was in good health. He was ready, if the right libretto presented itself, or the right librettist presented it, to extend the frontiers of his music further still into a totally new zone of musical experience. The kind of libretto which Strauss considered he needed for this purpose was not to Hofmannsthal's taste, but the poet was determined to ensure that no other librettist ousted him. He came up with an idea, far removed from the high tragic themes that the composer was demanding, but which he dangled in front of Strauss in the most tempting manner. This idea came to be called *Der Rosenkavalier*. It was to make Strauss a fortune and Hofmannsthal, too, a great deal of

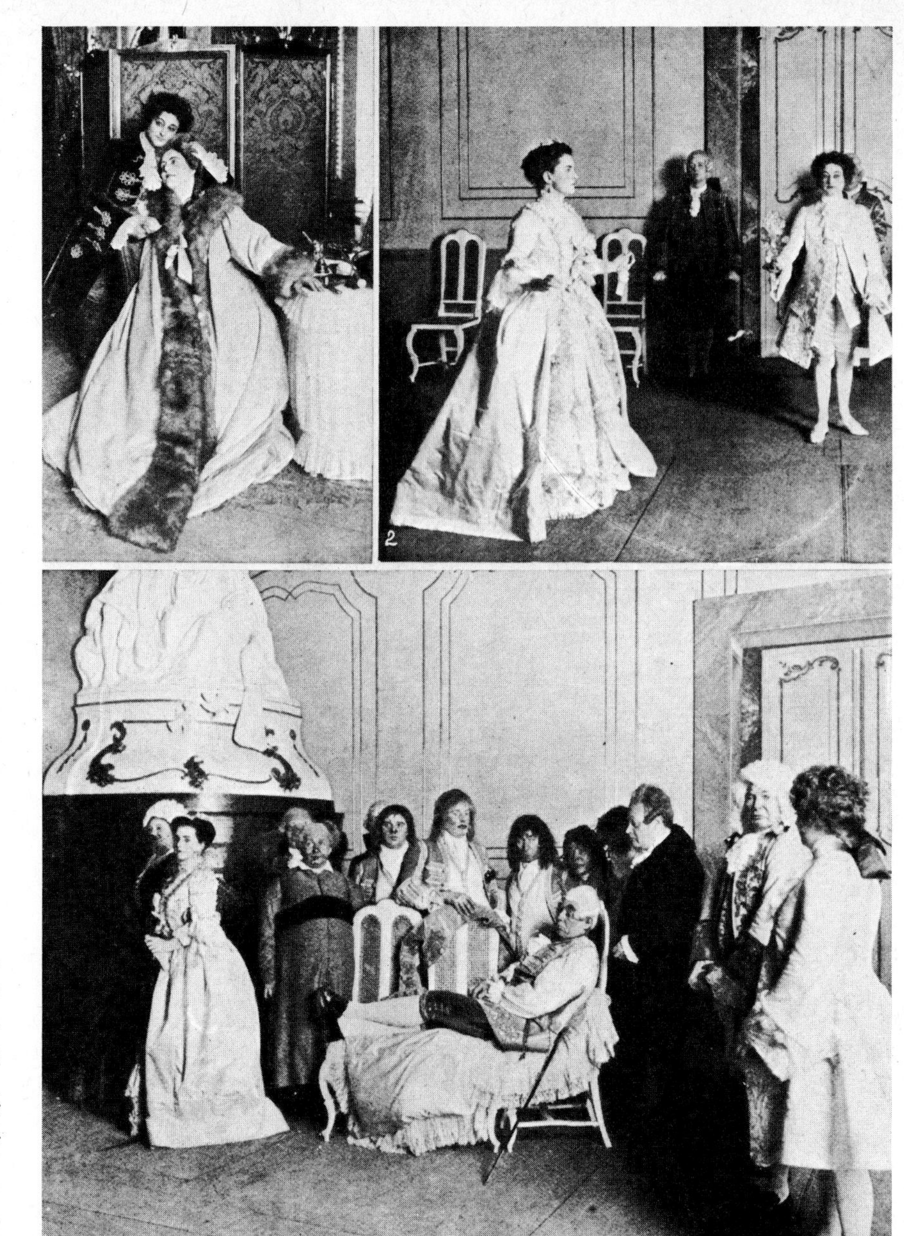

Three scenes from the original production of Der Rosenkavalier *in Dresden in 1911, showing (1) Eva von der Osten as Octavian and Margarete Siems as the Marschallin in the first scene of the opera; (2) the presentation of the Silver Rose with Minnie Nast as Sophie and Eva von der Osten as Octavian; (3) the scene of Ochs's pretended wound towards the end of Act II. Ochs is played by Carl Perron.*

Richard Mayr, the most celebrated Baron Ochs of all time, and the singer for whom Strauss wrote the part.

money, but it also finally diverted Strauss's inspiration from the road which led forwards from *Elektra*.

It now seems evident that Hofmannsthal overrode the composer's wishes by presenting him with a libretto so exquisite that he was unable to resist it. No composer in his senses would have done that. Hofmannsthal's first intimation of what he had in mind occurs in a letter to Strauss dated 11 February 1909. He was in Weimar, staying with Count Harry Kessler, a left-wing dilletante; a literary man in several languages; a printer, owner of the Cranach Press; later a kind of diplomat; and always one of Hofmannsthal's closest friends. On this day Hofmannsthal wrote: 'spent three quiet afternoons drafting the full and entirely original scenario for an opera, full of burlesque situations and characters with lively action, pellucid, almost like a pantomime . . . It contains two big parts, one for a baritone and another for a graceful girl dressed up as a man . . . Period: the old Vienna under the Empress Maria Thérèse'. This is it in a nutshell except that there is a third big part, for another soprano as magnificent and autocratic—and human—as the Empress herself, and as if to confirm the fact, that is what she is called in the opera, the Feldmarschallin Marie Thérèse.

It took Hofmannsthal and Strauss a few days under two years from this moment in a garden in Weimar for *Der Rosenkavalier* to appear before the world on the stage of the Dresden Opera. The work has become known for its gaiety and its waltzes to many tens of thousands of people who have never been inside an opera house, and although this aspect of the opera greatly appealed to Strauss, it did not interest Hofmannsthal. The first performance was given on 26 January 1911 and was even more of an event than *Elektra* had been on the same stage, almost exactly two years before. German Railways ran special '*Rosenkavalier* trains' from all over the Empire and within a few days both Strauss and Hofmannsthal were firmly established as the supreme masters of German—if not European—opera. (At this time Puccini had already presented five of his major works and was satisfying a popular Latin demand in his own way.)

There are several aspects of *Rosenkavalier* which make it a remarkable work. First of all there is no principal tenor (Strauss hated tenors), but there is one incidental tenor aria completely extra to the plot. The 'hero', Count Octavian Rofrano, is played by a mezzo-soprano and 'his' two lovers in this triangular plot are also sopranos. The truly male figure who thinks he figures all along as the hero is a Baron Ochs, a thoroughly endearing and comic character. This seedy country squire comes penniless to Vienna to marry a young girl whose father has recently been ennobled. Since Ochs's pedigree stretches back for many generations, it seems a good match. But Octavian falls in love with the young lady whose name is Sophie Faninal, and sets a trap

Königliches Opernhaus
Donnerstag, den 26. Januar 1911
Anfang 6 Uhr
Zum ersten Mal:
Der Rosenkavalier
Komödie für Musik in drei Aufzügen von Hugo von Hofmannsthal
Musik von Richard Strauss

Above: Playbill of the première.

Opposite above: Production team of Der Rosenkavalier *in Dresden, 1911. Standing behind: Max Reinhardt third from left, with Hofmannstahl next to him and Alfred Roller, bearded, the designer; and sitting, Strauss in the centre, and G.M.D. Ernst von Schuch right.*

Below: Scene from Act II of Paul Czinner's production of Der Rosenkavalier *with Sena Jurináč as Octavian, Erich Kunz as Faninal and Anneliese Rothenberger as Sophie.*

for Ochs so that he is completely discredited and has to go back to the country again, still a bachelor—but with access to more local girls than he can manage. Octavian gets Sophie, but this involves 'him' in having to dress up as a servant in two of the acts, and allowing him to escape seduction by Ochs, but only just. The undercurrents in this escapade have seldom been explored.

The Correspondence contains 43 pages about the creation of this opera, a short part of the book, but one of the most rewarding. We see exactly where and how the problems arose and how they were discussed, argued over and then dealt with. Not the least of these was when Strauss had finished setting and scoring Act II, and Hofmannsthal had not yet provided him with the words for any of Act III. Strauss's usually infallible timetable was considerably put out. But once he had these words, Strauss offered many helpful and constructive suggestions to Hofmannsthal, begging him all the time to clarify the words and the action more than he had been doing.

As soon as *Rosenkavalier*'s success was assured, its two creators set about exploiting their achievement. Strauss produced a number of suites and authorized arrangements for every kind of combination imaginable; while Hofmannsthal, who had already published the libretto as a play (so as to substantiate his copyright), wrote a film scenario to compliment rather than echo the opera story. Strauss wrote some additional music for this (silent) film, and it had a limited success between 1926–28. Alfred Roller, the designer of the opera sets at the première, also designed the film sets while Michael Bohnen, one of the celebrated interpreters of Ochs on the stage, took the acting part in the film. A long time afterwards, Paul Czinner filmed the 1960 Salzburg production of *Der Rosenkavalier* with Elisabeth Schwarzkopf as the Marschallin and Sena Jurináč as Octavian; this version is a brilliant and important living record of how the work was performed, at its best, half a century after its Dresden première.

While he was planning this opera, Hofmannsthal's active mind was already at work on two other subjects which, when he had disentangled them, became *Ariadne auf Naxos* ('Ariadne on Naxos') and *Die Frau ohne Schatten* ('The Woman without a shadow'). *Ariadne* started life as a one-act opera, pendant to a new translation of Molière's *Le Bourgeois Gentilhomme* by Hofmmansthal, for which Strauss also wrote some deliciously apt incidental music. The somewhat complicated production, involving as it did, a cast of actors, an orchestra of 23 and ten singers (but no chorus), needed the intimate atmosphere of a small theatre. This was found in Stuttgart, where the première took place on 25 October 1912. The old King of Württemberg, who was present, insisted on holding court for more than an hour during the interval after Molière's play. Those who had come for the acting were more tired than ever and some went home, while those who had come for the opera were almost too exhausted to appreciate it. Strauss realized that if the opera were ever to survive, it must be detached from the play, and suggested as much to Hofmannsthal, who at first would not hear of it.

At this point Hofmannsthal started to show a bitter and high-handed attitude towards Strauss which continued during much of their work on the next opera. His letter of 13 April 1916, might well have ended their collaboration had not Strauss been far more tolerant than the poet. The trouble was over the addition of a prelude to the opera of *Ariadne*, so as to make it a more acceptable length, in which Strauss wanted the role of the 'Composer' of the opera to be 'another Octavian', in other words a soprano dressed up as a man. 'Oh Lord, if only I could bring home to you completely the essence, the spiritual meaning of these characters. . . .' wrote Hofmannsthal, and ended his letter, 'I feel quite faint in mind and body to see us quite so far apart for once!' Strauss replied: 'Dear Herr von Hofmannsthal, Why do you always get so bitterly angry if for once we don't understand each other straight away? . . .' And this was the way it went, Strauss always willing to calm down the poet and even to make concessions, yet in the end he seemed to get very nearly everything he wanted!

The part of the Composer was eventually given to a soprano, and has turned out to be one of the most endearing Strauss wrote. Marie Gutheil-Schoder—said to be Strauss's favourite interpreter of Octavian in *Der Rosenkavalier*—was cast as the Composer in the revised version of *Ariadne*, but she failed to turn up to a number of rehearsals. Strauss agreed to hear a young soprano from Hamburg who was the

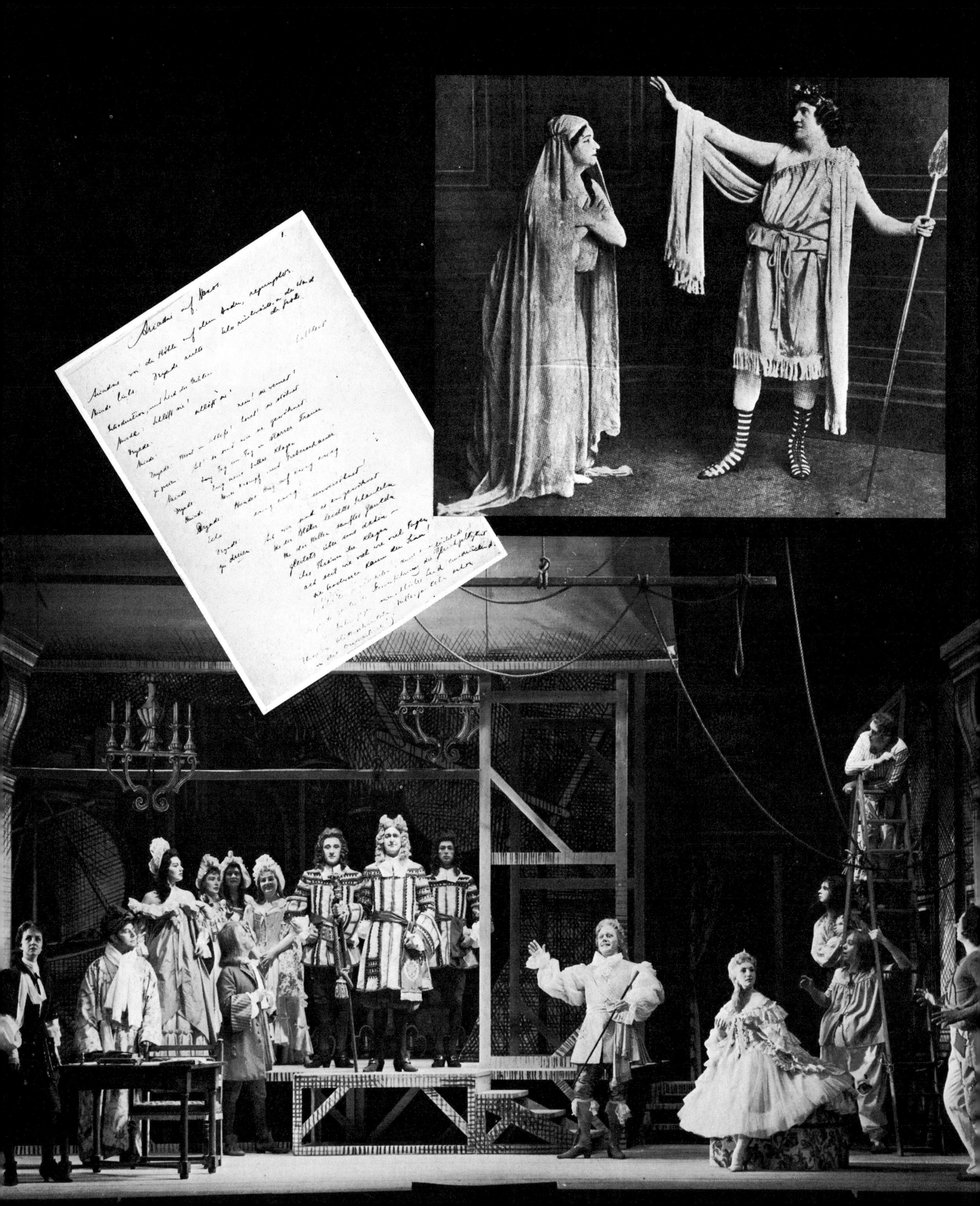

Graf Harry Kessler, German printer, man of letters, diplomat, and colleague of all the artistic giants before the First World War.

Opposite above left: First page of the text for Ariadne auf Naxos *(the opera) in Hofmannsthal's hand.*

Above right: The first London Ariadne (Eva von der Osten) and Bacchus (Otto Marak) posed in Grecian costume against Jacobean panelling. This was for the London première of the first version of the opera preceded by the play, in English, at His Majesty's Theatre, 1912, conducted by Beecham.

Below: The Prologue to Ariadne auf Naxos *by the London Sadler's Wells company in 1961, showing (extreme left) Elsie Morison as the composer, Alberto Remedios as the Tenor Singer, and sitting right, June Bronhill as Zerbinetta, in an imaginative set by Peter Rice.*

understudy. After only a few minutes, he insisted that she be cast in the role, irrespective of the feelings of Frau Gutheil. This young soprano was called Lotte Lehmann, and sang in the première in Vienna on 4 October 1916. This was the first of the four roles which she created for Strauss. She sang for and with him for twenty years.

There are two points about *Ariadne auf Naxos* which should not be overlooked. The plot combines two facets of Strauss's own character: the refined and the vulgar. The work involves two sets of characters which are paid to perform and to sing simultaneously. There is first, an opera company who perform the tragedy of *Ariadne on Naxos*, in which the Cretian heroine, abandoned on the island of Naxos by Theseus after helping him to escape the Minotaur, is comforted by the god Dionysus; as well as a Commedia dell'Arte troupe who perform the comedy *The Story of the Faithless Zerbinetta*. Both composer and poet found a great deal of sympathy with the situations which developed, and it has been somewhat unkindly suggested that Ariadne represents Hofmannsthal in everything that is pure and noble, high-minded and aristocratic, while Zerbinetta, her counterpart in the vulgar Italian troupe is none other than Strauss.

The work offers a fascinating study of Hofmannsthal's more abstruse calculations of character, for to him the two apparently unrelated stories together made a meaningful statement on the theme of Fidelity—one of his chief preoccupations. Strauss has certainly not tried to match his librettist's elaborate subtleties. On the contrary, he tried to force Hofmannsthal to simplify the plot and when he insisted on wrapping up one meaning in another, Strauss did his best to clarify matters with musical signposts. In fact Hofmannsthal's libretto for *Ariadne* seems more of an intellectual exercise for himself alone. If the feeble-minded audience could not follow him, that was just too bad. He wrote not for the idiots, but for the intelligentsia.

Strauss's achievement is of another kind. Despite the small orchestra of only twenty-three players, plus a harmonium and a piano, he obtains a very wide variety of textures, from the sound of a string quartet to the effect of a full symphony orchestra.

The adaptation saved the opera from obscurity, for the complete version with Molière's play is difficult to stage, while its expense is formidable. Nevertheless, Strauss always cherished a great fondness for the 'Bourgeois', and especially requested it to be staged again during his 85th birthday celebrations in Munich in 1949. Strauss also compiled a suite of the music from the play to be played as a concert item. It is pungently witty, being part based on Lully, part reflective of Strauss's own style and that of other composers in his best humorous vein

In 1912 Strauss was persuaded, much against his will, to compose a ballet for Diaghilev. The book, on the story of Joseph and Potiphar's wife, had already been written by Kessler and Hofmannsthal who had half-promised a Strauss score to the Russian impresario. Strauss was at first attracted by the story, though objected to having been let in for the job before he had himself agreed. When it came to setting the story, however, he found it quite unsympathetic and wrote: 'The chaste Joseph himself isn't at all up my street, and if a thing bores me I find it difficult to set it to music. This God-seeker Joseph—he's going to be a hell of an effort.' Unfortunately the score painfully shows Strauss's utter lack of interest; but he—and nobody else was ever able to boast this—secured full payment for his composition from Diaghilev in advance, of 5,000 gold marks. But Strauss never got paid his 6,000 gold francs for conducting it in Paris. Romain Rolland who attended the première of *Josephslegende*, as the ballet was called, has given this account of the occasion. 'The production of *Joseph* is the most magnificent that I have ever seen. In it the stage designer . . . and Fokine, the choreographer, eclipse the musician, although the latter has adapted himself to them with the litheness of a monkey. . . . Absolute harmony of the music with the slightest gesture or steps. For the rest, the music seemed to me of mediocre quality, docile, rather commonplace, but always amusing and of fine orchestral substance. . . . Strauss much aged, bloated, heavy and red. . . .'

The production came to Drury Lane Theatre at the end of June 1914. Strauss came over to conduct it. While in England, he also went to Oxford and received an honorary degree of Doctor of Music, saw to the good investment of most of his fortune on the London Stock Exchange, and left home again in early July. A month later, England and Germany were at war.

Chapter 6

Strauss and Opera-2

During the early performances of *Der Rosenkavalier*, in the Spring of 1911, Strauss and Hofmannsthal began work on the opera which was to follow *Ariadne auf Naxos*. It took Hofmannsthal some years to clarify his thoughts about the new work, and when he had done so, his correspondence with Strauss was sometimes concerned both with *Ariadne* and also with its successor, called *Die Frau ohne Schatten* ('The Woman without a Shadow'). Strauss used to abbreviate this name jokingly (but seldom to Hofmannsthal) when he referred to it as *Fr-o-Sch* which when run together in German means 'frog'. But there was nothing amusing about the creation of the work which caused much trouble and heartsearching. Strauss described it as 'a child of sorrow'. The war was in progress during its composition, his son Franz was in danger of being called up, then he became ill, Hofmannsthal had become a soldier, and everything seemed to be conspiring to thwart Strauss's personal plans. He was fifty.

Strauss, his wife and their son were together in San Martino di Castrozza in the Dolomites when the First World War broke out. They had some difficulty in forcing their way through Austrian troops in order to get back to Garmisch, but this was not the worst that happened during that week. 'On 1 August,' he wrote in his *Recollections and Reflections* 'the British confiscated my capital deposited with Edgar Speyer in London—the savings of thirty years. For a week I was very depressed: then I carried on with *The Woman without a Shadow* which I had just begun.'

During the War, the Correspondence tails off, but at the outset one is surprised at Strauss's tone to Hofmannsthal in his first letter since August 1914. 'Baron Franckenstein had already assured me . . . that you were no longer at the front but in safety at a quiet post. This was a great comfort to me. And now I think it may give you a little pleasure to know that the first four changes of scene of Act II are finished in draft.' In other words, the War and everything to do with it were just annoying interludes to take Hofmannsthal away from him and to disrupt their useful correspondence and occasional meetings. But Hofmannsthal, as a liaison officer, was far more concerned with and aware of the war, and had to drum it in to Strauss that things really had changed. 'I, for my part, cannot possibly travel to Germany, because I am on active service and nothing but sickness could support an application for leave.' They did not meet again until the end of April 1915, in Vienna, when clearly Hofmannsthal had been unable to concentrate on Act III, the most complex act of the whole opera, and one which really required his undivided attention. Strauss composed the act in September 1916 and he finished scoring it at the end of June 1917, so altogether the opera had taken a very long time, and was to have to wait even longer, until October 1919, before it reached the stage.

The Woman without a Shadow is probably Hofmannsthal's greatest intellectual achievement, and the most ambitious of all his libretti. But Strauss was constantly finding himself obliged to create musical means of simplifying Hofmannsthal's ideas which were often in danger of heaping one sort of confusion onto another. When he saw the opera performed in 1924, Romain Rolland wrote in his diary:

> A long performance, from 6–10. The work is full of picturesque and poetical happy thoughts; it even at times displays a pretty melodic vein; but it suffers from the German disease of musical development, of repetition. And Hofmannsthal's libretto affirms that writer's theatrical incompetency. His obscure thought trails an icy shadow. It weighs down the passion. Strauss suffers from his collaboration. His old spirit has gone to sleep, it's as if his blood has thickened. Bavarian phlegm.

But on the next evening Rolland watched Strauss conducting his *Domestica*, and his

Scene from the 1967 production of Die Frau ohne Schatten *at Covent Garden, with Hildegard Hillebrecht as the Empress and Regina Resnik as the Nurse in Act 1 of the opera. This photograph shows the extremely difficult problems encountered by the producer and designer to avoid the Empress being shown* with *a shadow until the critical moment at the end of the opera. Here, unfortunately, one has crept in. The remarkably evocative sets for this production were by Josef Swoboda.*

diary affirms that he had become 'the young Strauss once more, laughs with the timpani, takes pleasure in the joy he is unleashing.'

The Woman without a Shadow was not the success that its creators expected. It is a kind of fairy tale opera for grown-ups, extolling the desirability of producing children. It is very dark in texture and needs a huge orchestra. It also calls for particularly strong and special kinds of voices, although there is one part written in such a way that it is never today performed intact because it is too difficult and demanding. This character is called the *Amme* (or Nurse). She is the evil spirit of the story. When Georg Solti was given the opportunity to conduct the opera at Covent Garden in 1967, he began by considering the complete score, irrespective of 'usual' cuts. But he, too, found it necessary to make them in sections which are frankly unsingable. There are other moments that clutter or obscure the action and are best left out. In short, *The Woman without a Shadow*, the most heavily cut of all Strauss's operas, makes fearsome demands upon the designer's ingenuity, upon theatrical illusion and stage machinery. Strauss wrote 'In Vienna itself the strain imposed by the vocal parts and the difficulties over the sets, meant that the opera had to be withdrawn more often than it was performed,' and this was with a double cast of principal singers. After its Viennese première the next production, in Dresden, was a total failure, and when the work was mounted elsewhere, Strauss admitted that 'it was a serious blunder to entrust this opera, difficult as it was to cast and produce, to medium or small theatres. . . .' All the same, the magic of Strauss and Hofmannsthal can still work well in a good production of *The Woman without a Shadow*, conceived along the lavish lines of Victorian pantomime. There are many aspects of the huge and symbolically overblown opera which are exciting, gripping and amazingly beautiful.

The story concerns an Emperor and his young wife. She is the daughter of a spirit-king called Keikobad, who is never seen, though his 'signature' which opens the opera is often lurking in the background. Before the opera begins the Emperor has trapped her, in the shape of a gazelle, while hunting with his pet Falcon. She was wearing round her neck a talisman that allowed her to take whatever shape she wished and, being caught, she changed into a woman of such beauty that the Emperor at once fell in love with her and chased his Falcon away in a rage. However, the bird took with it the talisman. The fairy Empress presents problems. If she conceives before the twelfth moon she will be expelled from the spirit world and become a human; but if she fails to do so the Emperor pays the penalty for her excursion among mankind by being turned to stone, while she returns to Keikobad's domain. Her Nurse detests mankind and does everything possible to prevent the Empress from becoming human. At first one believes that the Nurse is acting strictly on behalf of Keikobad, but eventually we discover that—as in Mozart's 'Magic Flute'—what at first seems evil turns out to be good, and vice versa.

Hofmannsthal made of this partly-original story a wonderful, symbolic tale, but as his imagination blossomed, he began to overload the already substantial plot. There are two pairs of lovers, the Emperor and Empress on an exalted level, and a Dyer named Barak, and his Wife on a mundane level. A confusion arises even here from the title of the opera, for while Barak's wife is known in German as *Frau*, the *Frau* of the title, the one without a Shadow, is the Empress. Try as she does to conceive (in the Nurse's words the Emperor is 'nothing but a hunter and a lover; his nights are her day, his days her night') she cannot, and with each new moon she reports to one of Keikobad's Messengers that she is still not pregnant, and receives the same warning. On the other hand, Barak's Wife can easily conceive, but she is shrewish and unhappy and punishes her husband by sleeping alone. She feels that she has married below her station and covets a better existence than poor Barak—a noble and simple soul—can give her. So she and the Empress are at opposite poles.

Literally, since she is a fairy, the Empress has no shadow. As we know the Shadow means the power to conceive, since a human child, being cast in the same shape as the body from which it came, is in a sense a shadow. The key to the plot of the opera is the struggle for the Shadow between the Empress, who is trying to buy it from Barak's Wife, and the Nurse who is violently opposed to the idea, although she leads her charge into the hated world of humans, imagining that the Empress will find it as repulsive as she does. But the

Opposite: Die Frau ohne Schatten, *set designs for (above) the Falcon House and (below) the final scene, done somewhat in the style of Persian miniatures by Panos Aravantinos for the State Opera, Berlin production in 1920.*

Empress is intrigued, and as she learns to acquire compassion and a conscience, is thereby fit to become human—and pregnant. The fact that Barak's Wife goes through another kind of ordeal and also finds her true self, leads the opera to a happy ending, in which the two couples are surrounded by a chorus of the invisible spirits of children yet unborn.

Strauss uses large orchestral forces, as well as some unusual instruments (like a glass harmonica); he first thought of employing a smaller '*Ariadne*-sized' orchestra to accompany the superhuman elements, and the full-sized one for the remainder, with the two sometimes contrasted in weight and texture. Unfortunately this most interesting idea came to nothing.

Strauss often found himself at odds with Hofmannsthal during the composition of this opera. The poet's tone changed sharply round about the middle of 1916, during an argument concerning the revised version of *Ariadne* which we have already learnt about. It is clear from the correspondence that whenever Strauss tried to get Hofmannsthal to clarify the plot, Hofmannsthal grew impatient; he chose to ignore the fact that he was fully conversant with the story on all its various levels and symbolism, whereas Strauss was only too well aware that the average audience would be entirely at sea. Quite often he himself had to ask Hofmannsthal what he *really* meant by such and such a passage in the text, while at other times he was in disagreement with the motivation of some of the characters. One such passage concerns the voices of Barak's unborn children which issue from the mouths of fish, which his Wife is cooking for his supper. Barak comes in, sits down, and is given the fish to eat. Strauss objected strongly that this might—and very likely would—be taken literally to mean that Barak was eating his unborn children. Hofmannsthal poo-pooed the idea, but Strauss, by dint of persuasion, managed to get him to alter the scene.

The première took place in Vienna when Strauss was Co-Director there. It could scarcely have been put on at a less propitious time. A Viennese musician, the late Leo Wurmser, has told us how (as a boy) he attended the second performance in an impoverished Vienna where there was electricity rationing so that the opera had to be given in the afternoon. The once capital city of Europe was now shrunken to a magnificent jewel in the paste setting of a miniature and impotent republic. *The Woman without a Shadow*, conceived in that other world of 1914, was sadly out of place in 1919. From the start it seemed destined for failure; not until Clemens Krauss produced it at Salzburg and later on in Munich, did it achieve some of the acclaim which it deserved.

Neither Strauss nor Hofmannsthal seem to have appreciated the mood of post-War Europe so that they forged ahead as if nothing had happened. For Strauss this was because very little *had* happened to him; once he had got over the loss of his finances, he replanned his life and overcame the fears for his son's future. For Hofmannsthal, a return to civilian life was a wonderful change from military routine and discipline, and he merely carried on where he had left off. Their next joint work, produced at the Vienna State Opera in 1924, was a hotchpotch of Beethoven's *Ruins of Athens* and *Prometheus*. Strauss had contributed some essential fragments to fill in the naïve idea of the old Greek gods returned to earth, and it was a failure. Strauss was miscast as Co-Director with Franz Schalk an eminent conductor to whom he had entrusted the first performances of *The Woman Without a Shadow*, for two reasons. In the first place he was unequal to the intrigues which are as much part of that magnificent house as its bricks and mortar; and secondly he genuinely believed that the public wished to see his own operas and those he promoted on behalf of contemporary composers more than the traditional repertoire. In this he was very wrong, for Vienna is nothing if not traditional and reactionary in outlook and appeal.

Strauss faced a demonstration of no confidence. Some sterling supporters, including Hofmannsthal, rallied round but circumstances rather than people were against them. Strauss resigned in November 1924.

Hofmannsthal wrote to him '. . . it would be desirable that your general relations with Vienna (including those with the authorities etc.) should remain *tolerable*. . . . I take a calm and detached view of things and do not expect or wish you to take any particular steps, but I do ask you in our common interest not to contribute to anything which might make the rift between Vienna and you unbridgeable.' In other words: Don't rock the boat! In fact Strauss took the advice, though he may already have come to the same conclusion indepen-

Operntheater

Freitag den 10. Oktober 1919

Bei aufgehobenem Jahres-, Saison- und Stammsitzabonnement

Für das Pensions-Institut des Operntheaters

Bei erhöhten Preisen

Zum ersten Male:

Die Frau ohne Schatten

Oper in drei Akten von Hugo Hofmannsthal — Musik von **Richard Strauß**

Spielleitung: Hr. Breuer — Musikalische Leitung: Hr. Schalk

Der Kaiser	Hr. Oestvig
Die Kaiserin	Fr. Jeritza
Die Amme	Fr. Weidt
Geisterbote	Hr. Manowarda
Die Erscheinung eines Jünglings	Frl. Blei
Die Stimme des Falken	Frl. Mihacsek
Barak, der Färber	Hr. Mayr
Sein Weib	Frl. Lehmann
Der Einäugige (des Färbers Brüder)	Hr. Madin
Der Einarmige (des Färbers Brüder)	Hr. Betetto
Der Bucklige (des Färbers Brüder)	Hr. Arnold

Kaiserliche Diener, fremde Kinder, dienende Geister, die Stimmen der Wächter, Geisterstimmen

Entwürfe: Alfred Roller

Schauplätze der Handlung: I. Aufzug: Auf einer Terrasse über den kaiserlichen Gärten. — Färberhaus. — II. Aufzug: Färberhaus. — Wald vor dem Pavillon des Falkners. — Färberhaus. — Schlafgemach der Kaiserin. — Färberhaus. — III. Aufzug: Unterirdischer Kerker. — Geistertempel: Eingang. — Geistertempel: Inneres. — Landschaft im Geisterreich

Das Textbuch ist zum Preise von 8 Kronen, „Die Blätter des Operntheaters" zum Preise von 3 Kronen an der Kassa erhältlich

Nach dem zweiten Akt eine größere Pause

Der Beginn der Vorstellung sowie jedes Aktes wird durch ein Glockenzeichen bekanntgegeben

Kassen-Eröffnung vor ½5 Uhr — **Anfang 5 Uhr** — **Ende 9 Uhr**

Der Kartenverkauf findet heute statt für obige Vorstellung und für:

Samstag den 11. Die Frau ohne Schatten. Bei aufgehobenem Saison-Abonnement. Zu erhöhten Preisen. Für das Pensions-Institut des Operntheaters (Anfang 5 Uhr)

Sonntag den 12. Violetta (La Traviata) Für das Pensions-Institut des Operntheaters. Zu erhöhten Preisen (Anfang 6½ Uhr)

Weiterer Spielplan

Montag den 13. Die Königin von Saba (Anfang 6 Uhr)

Dienstag den 14. Die Frau ohne Schatten. Zu erhöhten Preisen. Für das Pensions-Institut des Operntheaters (Anfang 5 Uhr)

Preis 50 Heller

Above: Playbill for the première in Vienna.

Left: Final scene from the Covent Garden production, with Inge Borkh and Donald McIntyre as the Dyer and his wife, James King as the Emperor and Hildegard Hillebrecht as the Empress who has really found her shadow at last.

Below: Forbes Robinson as the Spirit Messenger at the opening of the 1967 Covent Garden production.

dently, and only a year after his resignation he was back again in Vienna as a guest conductor and—as usually happens in such circumstances—was even more popular than when he had been a Director. Franz Schalk remained at the Vienna Opera until his death in 1931, and although he and Strauss were never friends they appreciated each other's talents and recognized each other's value.

Throughout this unhappy time, Strauss and Hofmannsthal worked apart; Strauss writing and composing *Intermezzo*. But they resumed their partnership with *Die ägyptische Helena*, 'The Egyptian Helen' a two-act opera which fulfilled several of Strauss's ambitions. He wanted to compose another Grecian opera; to compose a lighter kind of work, more like an operetta; and to compose Helen of Troy and add her to his gallery of female portraits. Strauss had often urged Hofmannsthal to consider these possibilities, but now, when they started to take shape, the lighter aspects faded away to be replaced by far more portentous characters and situations. The person of an 'Omniscient Sea-Shell' certainly takes some beating even as a Hofmannsthal invention, and on the stage it can look all too much like a rococo television set.

The story tells how the real Helen was spirited away by the gods after the fall of Troy and transported to North Africa while her image remained behind in Greece. It is an interesting enough tale but it is, more or less, all over by the end of the first act, and with another act to go and precious little of real importance to say in it, the whole opera is out of balance. There are only two big numbers in it: Helen's Awakening and the opening of Act II after her second marriage night. Some Straussians have a fondness for the opera, but it is seldom performed, and is far from the best work of either Strauss or Hofmannsthal.

Their next opera—to be their last—was intended as 'another *Rosenkavalier*', an unfortunate key-phrase which had arisen in correspondence between them, but which got out to the public, who grew to expect nothing less. When it appeared, it was nothing like *Der Rosenkavalier* in characterization, period or comedy. The only common factor was the location in Vienna. *Arabella*, this new opera, tells of two daughters of an impoverished Count called Waldner. Because he and his wife cannot afford to bring them both out into society, only Arabella, the elder daughter, has this opportunity, while her sister Zdenka is made to dress as a boy and call herself Zdenko, Arabella's 'brother'. Among Arabella's admirers is one called Matteo, with whom Zdenka is infatuated. But Arabella ignores him despite bunches of flowers which arrive daily, while Zdenka writes him notes of encouragement which she signs with Arabella's name, so as to

Above: A scene from the Munich revival of Die ägyptische Helena *in Munich.*

Below: The same scene from the Dresden première.

Viorica Ursuleac, Richard Strauss and Alfred Jerger after the premiere of Arabella in Dresden. The two singers are shown in their costumes of Arabella and Mandryka, but unfortunately the success was not as great at the time as one might think from Strauss's expression.

prevent him from becoming disillusioned and going away. At a ball Zdenka seizes her opportunity and gives Matteo a key, telling him that it is to Arabella's room, and she expects him there at night. It is, of course, the key to Zdenka's room, and in the total darkness, which is part of the agreement, Matteo makes love to Zdenka while imagining that she is Arabella.

This is one of two plots which Hofmannsthal weaves together from two of his own early short stories. The other leg of the story deals with the unexpected arrival in the Waldner's hotel of a rich landowner from Transylvania called Mandryka. His father had been an old comrade of the Count's, and had received a picture of Arabella before he died. Now his heir has it, and has fallen in love with it. He arranges, without even seeing Arabella, to obtain her father's consent to marrying her, and in the solitary moment of humour in the opera, showers money on the old Count, who cannot believe his eyes. All goes well, for Arabella had seen Mandryka already, and had been very intrigued by him. But when Zdenka's misdemeanour comes to light and Matteo treats Arabella in an inexplicable manner (yet one in which he believes he has every right to do) Mandryka becomes insanely jealous and nearly packs his bags and leaves Vienna. At the right moment, Zdenka reveals that she is a woman and explains what she has done. So all ends happily when Arabella accepts the shame-faced Mandryka in a most beautiful final scene on the staircase of the hotel.

Strauss and Hofmannsthal enjoyed making this opera and had never been on such cordial terms. Save for the completion of the first act, the last scene of which had caused them some difficulties, all was finished on Hofmannsthal's side by the end of June 1929. On 10 July, Hofmannsthal wrote to Strauss, enclosing the revision, and on the 14th Strauss sent him a congratulatory telegram of thanks. But Hofmannsthal never saw it. On the morning of the 15th he died of a stroke, brought about by his elder son's suicide.

Strauss was so shattered by the news that he was unable to bring himself to attend Hofmannsthal's funeral, but he determined to leave the libretto exactly as it was, word for word, as an enduring monument to the man with whom he had worked and wrangled and succeeded and failed over the last 23 years: a lifetime of opera-making. *Arabella* was first staged in Dresden in 1933, with Clemens

München, Sonntag, 15. Februar 1953

In der neuen Inszenierung

Arabella

Lyrische Komödie in 3 Aufzügen von Hugo von Hofmannsthal

Musik von RICHARD STRAUSS

Musikalische Leitung: Rudolf Kempe — Inszenierung: Rudolf Hartmann
Bühnenbild: Helmut Jürgens — Kostüme: Rosemarie Jakameit

Rolle		Darsteller
Graf Waldner, Rittmeister a. D.		Max Proebstl
Adelaide, seine Frau		Irmgard Barth
Arabella	ihre Töchter	Maud Cunitz
Zdenka	ihre Töchter	Elfride Trötschel
Mandryka		Hermann Uhde
Matteo, Jägeroffizier		Lorenz Fehenberger
Graf Elemer	Verehrer der Arabella	Bernd Aldenhoff
Graf Dominik	Verehrer der Arabella	Karl Hoppe
Graf Lamoral	Verehrer der Arabella	Josef Knapp
Die Fiakermilli		Anny van Kruyswyk
Eine Kartenaufschlägerin		Ina Gerhein
Welko, Leibhusar des Mandryka		Walther Matthes
Djura	Diener des Mandryka	Walter Ehrengut
Jankel	Diener des Mandryka	Josef Schmidt
Ein Zimmerkellner		Emil Graf
Begleiterin der Arabella		Toni Eichner
Erster	Spieler	Erich Ringel
Zweiter	Spieler	Karl Mücke
Dritter	Spieler	Hermann Fries
Ein Arzt		August Wiedemann
Groom		Josefine Hetzenecker

Fiaker, Ballgäste, Hotelgäste, Kellner

Ort: Wien - Zeit: 1860

1. Akt: Salon in einem Stadthotel. 2. Akt: Ein öffentlicher Ballsaal.
3. Akt: Offener Raum mit Stiegenhaus im Hotel

Chöre: Herbert Erlenwein
Die Kostüme wurden in eigenen Werkstätten unter Lovis Révy hergestellt
Maskenbildner: Georg Rasche - Anfertigung der Dekorationen: Ludwig Hornsteiner
Technische Oberleitung: Albert Rall - Technische Einrichtung: Hans Herrmann
Beleuchtung: Josef Dusch und Ludwig Bourdillon
Inspektion: Anton Hackel und Martin Brucklachner - Souffleuse: Eva Hamer

Anfang 19 Uhr — **Pause nach dem 1. Aufzug** — **Ende 22 Uhr**

Erfrischungsraum gegenüber der Eintrittskartenkasse

Verkaufszeiten: Montag mit Samstag 9—13 Uhr und 16—18 Uhr, Sonn- und Feiertage 9—13 Uhr
Abendkasse 1 Stunde vor Vorstellungsbeginn

Orientieren Sie sich telefonisch im Kundendienst der Post (Rufnummer 594)
über den Spielplan und evtl. Spielplanänderungen

Left: The curtain call after the first night of Arabella *at Covent Garden in 1934, with the original Dresden cast. This picture shows Viorica Ursuleac in the centre, about to be joined by the principal male singers in the company. The visit of the Dresden company coincided with Strauss's 70th birthday, and there was an extra performance of* Arabella *in London to celebrate it.*

Above: Cast of the 1953 Munich revival of Arabella, *which was brought to London in the autumn of that year—the first time* Arabella *had been heard in London since 1934.*

Krauss conducting and his wife Viorica Ursuleac as Arabella. But it failed to attract the kind of support which Strauss expected. It was only after 1945 that *Arabella* began to win success—largely thanks to the soprano Lisa Della Casa and her graceful interpretation of the name-part. Providing the heroine can be adequately cast, the opera will continue to maintain a strong position in the Strauss canon.

It is curious to find that there is a touch of Hofmannsthal's imagination in every opera but one which Strauss composed after the poet's death, and sometimes far more than that. The one exception is *Die schweigsame Frau*, 'The Silent Woman'. Hofmannsthal had the full sweep of *Die Liebe der Danae* in his mind before the end of the 1920s; he almost invented the Countess in *Capriccio*; he toyed with the idea of Daphne and her metamorphosis; he got more than one idea of *Friedenstag* from his wartime experiences. So whereas Hofmannsthal was mercifully removed from Austria before the Nazis were able to threaten him for his Jewish blood he indirectly influenced Strauss's later output, right to the end: a fitting state of affairs for the most interesting and by far the most subtle and imaginative opera librettist of our time.

When Hofmannsthal died, Strauss's methods of work were so sure and so well tried as to defy change, even such a disastrous event as the loss of his librettist. We have seen how his wife had bullied him into dividing each day, as profitably as possible when he was at home with a composition to get on with. The programme ensured delivery of scores on schedule and even when he was alone in his study at Garmisch, where the very view is an inspiration to beauty and to endeavour, Strauss pursued the same methods. Many composers hack out their ideas on the piano and work out their harmonies there with music paper on the rest, producing the short score in this way, from the piano arrangement or else direct. Strauss did not compose at the piano. He did it all mentally, making his short score with the aid of scribbles which represented ideas as they occurred to him in the course of reading through the libretto. It must be said that on rare occasions he failed to read the words in the right context and sometimes even set the stage directions to music. In a letter to Hofmannsthal on New Year's Eve 1928 he wrote, à propos the 'Egyptian Helen':

There now: I've again set a stage direction to music! But since it has turned out a pretty vocal phrase [and here he quotes it] I want to ask if instead of 'drowsy and overcome by sleep' you couldn't write some other suitable words to music so I don't have to cut out the tune.'

Hofmannsthal obligingly replied that he would see to it that the passage was saved. Every phrase Strauss set, once there, was solidly part of the fabric, for, except in the case of *Intermezzo*, Strauss composed each act of an opera on the basis of full symphonic structure.

Strauss was celebrated for the delicacy and accuracy of his musical caligraphy. There was hardly ever a mistake in the whole of a full score, which he might have written out over several months of almost continuous work, between concerts and opera performances. While most composers and music start at the foot of the page with the bass parts upon which a composition rests, Strauss began at the top and worked downwards, more often than not inventing the orchestration as he went along. This is nothing short of miraculous; when asked by Gregor why he worked in this way, he replied that if he wrote the notes from the bottom upwards, he would probably smudge the ink.

Strauss said that 'spiritual excitement, anger and annoyance' were more likely to inspire him than good temper and a mind open to any mood which came along. He emphasized that this was very much the way in which the Composer in *Ariadne* got hold of the *Du Venussohn* theme in the Prologue, by having an argument with a lackey and then by being delighted at seeing the Tenor biffing his Wigmaker for doing a bad job. Yet not everybody finds slight emotional upsets a stimulus to clear thinking.

When datelines were set, they were Strauss's own. Commissions with time limits imposed from outside never inspired him, and he was then obliged to 'note-spin'. Nobody could distinguish this better than he but when all went well, he enjoyed composition—and especially orchestration—so much that it was 'pure pleasure'. He gave thanks that he was able to pursue a profession which gave him such great satisfaction; when he heard other composers for whom composition was a long drawn out process, and who sometimes lost all pleasure in what they were doing he was frankly incredulous. Strauss once declared that he composed everywhere he went, and we know that one of the most important melodies for *Der Rosenkavalier* was scribbled on the back of a telegram during a skat game.

Clemens Krauss and Strauss outside the Festival Theatre, Salzburg in 1933.

Strauss's extraordinary technique which enabled him to 'note-spin' with such proficiency was the secret of the fluency with which he composed when he was inspired. Karl Böhm who saw Strauss's original jottings at first reading among and beside the words for *Daphne* in Gregor's final libretto, was astonished, when he compared them with the finished score, to find that Strauss had acted on them completely. 'Strauss had jotted down notes concerning rhythms, and the tonality too as a rule, and there were precise indications of the musical form where several characters sang together. All this happened in scarcely a moment longer than it took to read the words, a complete creative activity.'

He was able to put his ideas straight onto the paper without the aid of a piano, because, for the most part, they had been gestating and maturing in his mind for some time. The same was true of Hofmannsthal, whose literary ideas fermented in his brain until he found them 'safe'. Strauss said once:

> I often write down a motif or a melody, then put it away for a year. When I return to it I find that quite unconsciously something in me—the imagination—has been at work on it.

And he also said:

> Before I note down even the slightest sketch for an opera I allow the text to permeate my mind for at least six months and take root within me, so that I am wholly familiar with the situations and characters.

To some extent he learnt the technique from Hofmannsthal and later applied it when sheer inspiration ceased to be there to guide him. When we recall that he said he was already composing *Salome* on the way out from seeing the play, there clearly was a change in his methods in later life. Other indications as to how he composed have been left by Strauss:

> Two bars of a melody occur to me spontaneously so I spin it out and write a few more bars, but soon I sense inadequacies, and I lay one foundation stone after another until at last I find the right version. That sometimes takes a long time, a very long time. A melody which seems to have been born in a moment is almost always the result of laborious work. . . .

And about his songs:

> Musical ideas have prepared themselves in me—God knows why—and when, as it were, the barrel is full, a song appears in the twinkling of an eye as soon as I come across a poem more or less corresponding to the subject of the imaginary song while glancing through a book of poetry. If, however, the flint does not strike a spark at the decisive moment, if I find no poem corresponding to the subject which exists in my sub-conscious mind, then the creative urge has to be re-channelled to the setting of some other poem which I think lends itself to music. It goes slowly, though, because the music which had developed spontaneously has to be reshaped if it is to see the light of day. I resort to artifice. . . .

Strauss was fastidiously methodical and his writing table at Garmisch was a perfect model of neatness. All his manuscripts and sketch books were precisely indexed and docketed so that he might refer to one of his melodies which he had put 'on ice'. No telephone calls disturbed him and no message, however important, was allowed to reach him until he had emerged for a meal. All composition was done at Garmisch and during the middle of his life when he was in Berlin the scoring was done there. Scoring was such a pleasure that it was as good as a relaxation after the full, mental concentration which composition involved. He lived up to his own maxim that a composer must never allow his ideas to run away with him, that he must be in complete command of his own invention. 'The composer of Tristan had a head that was as cold as marble!' With all the immense emotion in Wagner's opera, it would have been the easiest, as well as the most disastrous thing in the world for the composer to have let it run away with him. Strauss appreciated this only too well, and this accounts for reports of him which conclude that he was heartless and disinterested in what he was doing. Only the onlookers were unaware of what was involved.

The same restrained care governed his work as a conductor; in fact, his quiet control before a performance was often commented on unfairly. As he became older, he used to ensure that the rehearsals had all been taken for him and then arrived at the opera house, perhaps only a minute before the performance was due to start. He would keep the audience waiting expectantly for another couple of minutes or so (a long time once the lights have been dimmed), and then would go straight onto the rostrum and give the downbeat. After a first night, he would generally sit calmly in his dressing-room (while the cast and management were excitedly talking and running about) attending very systematically to a large pile of autograph books. Afterwards he played skat, for preference, if he saw no way out of attending a first-night party. He disliked all social events, as did his wife. It is said that they used to vie with each other in how many invitations they turned down in a season. Strauss's self-ordered way of life had no part in the social scene. He had a place for everything, and everything had to be in its place, or else he would never have been able to manage the large output which was his contribution to German and European music.

Chapter 7

Strauss and Politics

Above: Kaiser Wilhelm II whose singularly autocratic views on music are described on this page

Left: Female support for the Führer at the opening of the Olympic Games in Berlin in 1936, for which Strauss wrote a special Hymn.

The composer's political record during the Nazi period has earned him much criticism. As we shall see, however, while he may sometimes have been stupid and sometimes wary in the interests of his family, he never in any important sense 'collaborated' with the regime and never for one moment shared or approved its ethos or objectives. In fact, while he shared with most of his contemporaries in Europe strong sentiments of patriotism, Strauss was not in the least politically minded. He lived and worked for music and for music alone, and always exerted himself to promote the well being of his country's music. Sometimes this involved him unwittingly or externally in politics and politicians and while his sheer naïvety about Nazi intentions is sometimes culpable it was by no means unique in Germany.

We find Strauss on the fringe of politics at the beginning of the century when he was General Music Director at the Court of Kaiser Wilhelm II. He occasioned some anxiety in Court circles, and a permanent antipathy on the part of the Empress with his operas *Salome*, *Elektra* and *Der Rosenkavalier*. She considered them to be indecent and did her best to have them withdrawn from the Berlin Opera. Other men would have taken more trouble than Strauss did to placate his royal enemy, but this was not his way. As a senior Court musician he provided several military pieces as part of his job: four marches to grace Prussian parades, a soldier's chorus and a bombastic brass flourish, all in the year 1909 (the only compositions which he turned out between *Elektra* and *Der Rosenkavalier*). Two of the marches were dedicated to the Kaiser, in the somewhat fulsome address required by German court etiquette which composer's had felt it polite to use ever since the great Bach had written the dedications to the King of Poland and the Duke of Saxony.

But Strauss was well aware that the Kaiser was an artistic philistine, and he had many an argument with him about music. He used to enjoy himself by expressing his own views, quite contradictory to those of his monarch, and still remaining within the bounds of courtly politeness. After a performance of Weber's *Freischütz*, which Strauss had conducted, the Kaiser sent for him and in conversation referred to a modern work by the Prussian composer von Schillings.

Kaiser: So you are another of these modern composers. It was detestable that work of Schillings there isn't an ounce of melody in it.
Strauss: It may be, Your Majesty, that the melody in it is concealed behind its polyphony.
Kaiser: You are one of the worst [with a disagreeable frown].
Strauss is silent
Kaiser: All modern music is worthless, there isn't an ounce of melody in it [repeating himself]. I prefer *Freischütz*.
Strauss: Your Majesty, I also prefer *Freischütz*.

In any case Strauss was a Bavarian, and all Bavarians, with their Austrian affinities, dislike and mistrust the natives of Northern Germany, and the Prussians in particular. Bavarians are broad-minded, easy going, extrovert, and possess some sense of humour. They tend to regard Prussians as pig-headed, literal minded, fond of discipline, and without any element of humour. Actually this is a slander on native Berliners but although his conducting career kept him at the Prussian capital, Strauss did not belong there temperamentally, and always went home to the South whenever he could.

A letter to Hofmannsthal in the first winter of the 1914–18 War had this to say of the political climate of Germany at war:

It is sad enough that mature and serious artists like ourselves whose work remains true to artistic ideals, must pay so much heed to people for whom this great epoch serves merely as a pretext for bringing their mediocre products into the open, who seize the opportunity to decry real artists as hollow aesthetes and bad patriots. . . . It is sickening to read in the papers about the regeneration of German Art . . . or to read how Young Germany is to emerge cleansed and purified from this 'glorious' war, when in fact one must be thankful if the poor blighters are at least cleansed of their lice and bedbugs and cured of their infections and once more weaned from murder!

Throughout the Nazi period, Strauss might have found himself in as deep water for uttering such a statement as indeed he was to be in 1935 when he criticized Nazi Germany in a letter to his next librettist, the Jew Stefan Zweig. As we shall see, this episode displayed a naïvety that is barely credible but Strauss has the same single-minded concentration on his own business as a musician even among the court and intriguers of the imperial epoch.

From his own point of view, his only enemies were musicians who had either failed to match his own abilities, or who felt themselves offended by his undoubted hauteur. There are plenty of criticisms of Strauss for being pompous and overbearing, and, on occasion, exceedingly rude. He was very tall, and was often obliged to stoop slightly when talking to a shorter person; he was conscious of his own standing in the musical world, and rather enjoyed it; and his sly sense of humour generally got the better of him whenever he was in the company of Prussians or of anybody who took altogether seriously anything which he said. But he could not bear trivialities or time-wasting. His mind was never still, and like most intelligent people he prefered to be in the company of his own kind. As a result Strauss became very easily bored, and frequently made this quite clear to the assembled company. Such was his standing at the end of the First World War, that he was requested, even urged, by the caretaker management of the newly christened 'State Opera' to take it over and look after it during the uncertain times through which Germany was passing. This included a revolution in Berlin itself which followed immediately after the Armistice in November 1918. All this was something completely outside Strauss's life. He had recently resigned from the Opera in Berlin after a disagreement with the old administration, but now that others had taken its place, and he did not have to deal with the same people, he decided to return. Although there is no record of how Strauss behaved in Berlin while the revolution was in progress, it is extremely doubtful that he took much account of it. In almost any situation his motto was business as usual, and one can imagine him travelling the turbulent streets between his apartment and the Opera House oblivious of the unrest. If Strauss's actions in Berlin appear selfish, let us remember that he really wished to go back to Garmisch and work on his *Intermezzo*. Instead, he remained at the Opera because he considered that much worse influences than he might take over in Berlin. With the conductorship of the Staatskapelle (formerly the Royal Court Orchestra) as an additional duty, he was, for a year, lynch-pin for the organization which he had served faithfully enough

German munition workers (and one sailor) at the beginning of the German revolution in Berlin in November 1918, when they marched under the Red Flag against the temporary government.

for the past 20 years. Undoubtedly this gave German musicians the comforting feeling that whatever else had changed in the upheaval and aftermath of war, Richard Strauss was still there to represent the strength of German music and was even in control. This was not the last time that Strauss was to set aside his own plans in the service, as he conceived it, of German music.

Strauss was 54 when the First World War ended, and he had spent most of the war years either in revising *Ariadne* and in composing its new Prologue, or in creating the music for *Die Frau ohne Schatten*, both as far away from war and wartime as can be imagined. Nevertheless, he wrote several times to Hofmannsthal that in his opinion it was *work* which was essential for the moral welfare of everyone in wartime; as he had been born a musician, this was his work: let others do what suited them best. He entirely dissociated himself from propaganda and refused to speak or to write about the war. He also refrained very pointedly from adding his name to a document, gladly subscribed by many German artists, which decried foreigners and their culture. Among Strauss's most admired friends was the French poet Romain Rolland who, despite the nationalist hysteria engendered by the War did not change his positive views about Germany's culture. From neutral Switzerland he had even published an idealistic manifesto, dissociating himself from the War and its first line goes:

> To my enemies: they may hate me, but they will not succeed in teaching me to hate.

This inspired the French nation to condemn him as 'the only pacifist Frenchman', especially when he had a great deal to say in favour of German culture. When, shortly afterwards, he discovered that certain German atrocities which he had refused to believe in had actually happened, he wrote another paper that condemned those responsible. Now the full weight of German venom descended upon Rolland, and he found himself alienated from both sides.

He and Strauss continued their friendship during the War and if they had little in common as people, they were both politically naive, and shared the same high artistic ideals, about the only human qualities which can transcend national boundaries and international disputes. In 1917 Strauss wrote to Rolland, inviting him to visit him in Garmisch. Even Rolland was amazed at this. 'Reverse the situation' he exclaimed. 'A German invited to France, it would be like one of Napoleon's soldiers in besieged Saragossa!' They seem not to have corresponded again until 1924; but when in 1926, on Rolland's 60th birthday, a number of his friends collectively produced a liber amicorum Strauss subscribed a song to words by Goethe, with the following dedication:

> To the great poet and highly esteemed friend
> The heroic fighter against all the wicked powers working for the destruction of Europe
> With the expression of my deepest sympathy and sincere admiration.

When one considers the development of Strauss's views on 'the authorities', and the kind of life, dedicated to art and contemptuous of politics, that he was used to, it is hardly surprising that his behaviour accorded ill with Nazi precepts when Hitler's party came into power. Thanks to his international standing, Strauss seemed likely to be a valuable propaganda tool for them. He commanded the respect of influential people, musicians and the press all over the world, but he was, from Hitler's and Goebbel's point of view, too wrapped up in his work to exploit these valuable assets to full effect. Accordingly, to give him a platform from which to deploy his prestige in the service of the Reich, the title and office of President of the Reich's Chamber of Music was conferred upon him in November 1933, without the formality of an invitation. Strauss was simply not given any opportunity to refuse this 'honour'. It was followed on his 70th birthday by autographed pictures of Hitler and Goebbels, in silver frames. Such obvious marks of favour, completely unlooked for by the composer himself, inevitably suggested to the outside world that the 'grand old man' of German music supported Nazism. We get a more accurate hint as to Strauss's own views in the matter in the answers he made on the form issued in connection with his appointment to the presidency of the Chamber of Music. Officialdom, trying to catch up with its paper work, demanded not only details of his professional career, but also the names of two well-known composers prepared to vouch for him. Contemptuously, Strauss recommended the bureaucrat to approach 'Wolfgang Amadeus Mozart and Richard Wagner' as referees for his musical competence.

This kind of thing amused Strauss, it also irritated the authorities, but it did not alter the view of the international community that Strauss was now a fully fledged Nazi official; in some quarters the stigma has persisted until the present time. Strauss greeted the title with some dismay but, it must be admitted, did not protest. He consoled himself with the thought that he might at least be more willing than others he knew to work towards a betterment of conditions of musicians in Germany. Strauss's Vice-President of the Chamber was Wilhelm Furtwängler, upon whom fell a lot of administrative work simply because Strauss made himself as inaccessible as possible in Garmisch. In addition, Furtwängler took his duties extremely seriously, and made something of a nuisance of himself among the true bureaucrats. Later he had conferred on him—without prior warning from Goering—the title of Prussian State Councillor, which never happened to Strauss.

Shortly after his appointment in December 1933, he chose to set to music a poem (anonymous) in which the poet calls on the little stream to be his leader. In the text appear the words '. . . *mein Führer*, *mein Führer*, *mein Führer sein!*' Of course, despite Hitler's appropriation of the term, in German the word '*Führer*' simply means 'Leader'; in English however it has only one connotation and as a result Strauss's reputation has been further blackened by ignorant or malicious commentators. It is doubtful whether Strauss saw anything particularly political about his charming little song, entitled *Das Bächlein* and only a few months later in early 1934, he was to be heard describing the Nazi heirarchy as 'that unsavoury Hitler and his shabby gang of Philistine myrmidons'. Perhaps this illustrates as well as anything the dual nature of Strauss's attitude to people: how he appeared to be on one side when a moment later he said something which convincingly showed that he was siding with the other. In fact he was on his *own* side, the Musicians' side, and genuinely quite divorced from partisanship. Photographs of

A senior Nazi Party meeting being addressed by Dr Josef Goebbels in November 1934 in Berlin, on the occasion of the recently formed Department of Culture in the Third Reich. In the front row are: second from left Goering, von Papen, Hitler and, across the gangway, Minister Funk. Next but one to Funk is Wilhelm Furtwängler and then Richard Strauss, both of whom are understandably looking very bored.

The only existing picture from the première of Die schweigsame Frau *in Dresden in 1935, which was taken off by order of the Nazis on account of its Jewish librettist. The characters shown here are, Henry (Martin Kremer), Morosus (Friedrich Plaschke) and Aminta (Maria Cebotari).*

Strauss shaking hands with Nazi leaders may seem abhorrent in retrospect but then there are pictures of King Edward VIII of England and Mrs Simpson shaking hands with Hitler.

Moreover, even when he held the office of Music President, Strauss ignored the prohibition on communicating with Jews, and openly wrote to Jewish friends both inside and outside the Reich. Indeed, from 1932 onwards, he was actually working with one on his next opera, *Die schweigsame Frau* ('The Silent Woman'). The librettist, Stefan Zweig, had been very warmly recommended to Strauss in 1929, as Hofmannsthal's successor. He produced a libretto which appealed very much to the composer. It was based on Ben Jonson's play *Epicœne* and has strong similarities to Donizetti's *Don Pasquale*. Once again Dresden was chosen as the right theatre for the première and a new generation of Strauss singers was picked to take part in his first truly comic opera devoid of satire.

The opera is set in London in 1780 and tells of an old English sea captain, called Morosus, a confirmed bachelor, who is persuaded to think seriously of marriage by a Figaro-like character (who is also his barber).

Morosus' nephew, Henry, arrives home from abroad with a troupe of Italian singers, which astonishes and displeases the old man; when they start singing he is appalled. But with the help of the Barber and some costumes, three of the company appear disguised before Morosus as candidates for his marriage bed. The one he likes best is in reality Henry's wife —Henry having concealed the marriage so as not to be disinherited by his uncle. 'Timida', as the pretty girl calls herself, wins the old man's approval, and they go through a ceremony of marriage in which two members of the opera company act as 'priest' and 'clerk'. But no sooner is the ceremony over than Timida starts to rant and rave, and so upsets Morosus with her dreadful noise, that he is beside himself. Throughout the second act he is doing everything he can to obtain a divorce. After a lengthy and importantly comic legal wrangle, everything is put to rights and Morosus is desperately relieved at being freed from his dreadful 'wife'. In his delight he confirms Henry as his heir and reflects that he has never felt better in all his life. The best thing about a pretty woman, he says, is knowing that she is somebody else's wife.

In 1933 Strauss damaged his personal reputation critically when he conducted *Parsifal* at Bayreuth in place of Toscanini; the great Italian had insulted Hitler and failed to honour his contract on humanitarian grounds. Strauss stepped in to save the production. Many artistic people then and since regarded this as an act wholly in keeping with Nazi principles; it was not; but even the most sympathetic observer must feel that here Strauss was allowing his devotion to art to go too far. While at Bayreuth he took the opportunity to get official agreement from Goebbels to go ahead with the production of *Die schweigsame Frau* despite Zweig's known Jewish background. For since September 1933, all theatres and music in the Reich had come under the direct control of Goebbels as Propaganda Minister. After a good deal of misunderstanding over the libretto when the Nazis entirely failed to discover anything racially objectionable in it at all, Strauss was given Goebbels's assurance that all was well.

The more one reflects on Strauss's strange, and at times apparently ambivalent, stance during the Nazi period, the more one feels that his prime fault was to have been a totally self-motivated individual in an age of ideological commitment. He did not at one point decide to collaborate and at another to resign from it all; at the deepest level of his personality he was unable to grasp the idea that anything could take precedence over music. At Bayreuth he saw only a great musical event in jeopardy and the hard work of hundreds of professional colleagues threatened. Two years later, Reichsminister Goebbels was to learn that even his 'principles' were irrelevant in the Straussian code which placed artists far above politicians. The Dresden production of *The Silent Woman* taught the Nazi régime that the appointment of Strauss to high office in the Reich's artistic hierarchy was not the simple propaganda stroke they had imagined, but was to involve them too in compromise. For bolstering his reputation with official sanction gave him real power. He now used it to champion an artistic colleague.

A short time before the opening of the opera in June 1935, Strauss was playing skat in the lounge of his Dresden hotel, when he suddenly asked to see a proof of the poster for the première. After some prevarication, it was brought to him and when he saw it he flew into a towering rage. He took his pen and inserted Zweig's name, which had been omitted (nobody knows who tipped him off about this, but clearly somebody had done). He then declared that unless the posters were printed again with Zweig's name as large as Hofmannsthal's name had been on the playbill for *Der Rosenkavalier*, he would leave and the première might continue without him. The poster was altered, but the Gestapo got to hear of it and informed Hitler. He cancelled his intention to be present and so did Goebbels.

Artistically speaking, Strauss was delighted with the opening performance. 'Your libretto is perfect, if only for the 21st Century' he had written to Zweig, and certainly most of the audience enjoyed the good humour, while others relished the slightly cruel baiting of Morosus. Zweig was not there, but a large cohort of black-shirts were. The change in the constitution and mood of the audience was very noticeable. Afterwards Strauss wrote Zweig the same kind of critical letter as he had written to Hofmannsthal over twenty years earlier (see pages 88–90) during the other war. But this time his lack of tact—or merely his indifference—was to bring about the most serious consequences to Strauss. His often quoted letter to Zweig was intercepted by the Gestapo and sent to Hitler, who read these words:

> Do you think that Mozart deliberately composed in an Aryan manner? For me there are only two categories of human beings: the talented and the untalented. And for me the populace only exists from the moment when it becomes an audience. It's all the same to me whether they are Chinese, Upper Bavarians, New Zealanders or Berliners, so long as they've paid the full price at the box-office.

Oddly enough, Berlioz had once said almost the same thing, so the sentiment which Strauss expressed was not even original. As a result of this direct insult to the State and total lack of responsibility in the eyes of the German government, as well as what they viewed as the unscrupulous advantage he had taken of his office so as to work with a non-Aryan and make the most out of it, Hitler ordered that the opera *The Silent Woman* was to be taken off the Dresden stage, and further productions of it in the Reich were to be banned. This was the bitterest blow that Strauss ever suffered, and he never fully understood why. A few days later, when he had returned to Garmisch in utter depression,

Above: Stefan Zweig, the Austrian-Jewish librettist of Die schweigsame Frau *and, to a large degree, of* Friedenstag, *as well as the proposer of the basic idea inherent in* Capriccio. *Zweig was a man of enormous sensibility and originality. He posessed one of the finest private collections of autographs in Europe, but it was plundered, dispersed and destroyed by the Nazis when they raided his Salzburg house.*

Right: Characteristic magazine cover at the time of the 1936 Olympic Games in Germany.

1936

2. SONDERHEFT

PREIS 1 MARK

Berliner Illustrirte Zeitung

BERICHT
in Wort und Bild

„Die 16 olympischen Tage"

Above: The Bayreuth Festival of 1937 was patronized by Hitler, and he is seen here being welcomed by Winifred Wagner (the composer's daughter-in-law) before a performance of Parsifal *which was conducted by Furtwängler.*

Left: Viorica Ursuleac as Countess Madeleine in the last scene of Capriccio, *which she sang at the première.*

he received a visit from one of Goebbel's staff who informed him that he must relinquish his office of President 'on grounds of ill-health'. Strauss wrote a memorandum which he kept among his private papers, and which was never seen by anybody else until after his death. A pity, because in it he vindicates his behaviour by the utmost lack of comprehension about what was going on in Germany.

However, in one respect he did sense the terrible implications of Nazism and when they threatened his own family he did not hesitate to write a letter which finally blackened his own good name. The letter was to Hitler and it was a gesture of total appeasement. In 1924 his son Franz had married a Jewess called Alice Grab, so that Strauss's grandsons were half-Jewish. They had to be saved at whatever cost to their famous grandfather's reputation. Strauss did save them and at no time were they actually threatened with deportation, but Martin Bormann for one was furious at Strauss's capitulation and tried to make an example of him. Strauss killed his own reputation, certainly, but never as badly as the writings of Marek, or the film by Russell, have attempted to make out by their wilful malice and racial prejudices in a situation that still seems to be fraught with misunderstandings and bias.

For a year Strauss was forbidden to appear in public in the Reich. He went abroad and conducted his operas in Italy, where Mussolini was thoroughly in favour of *The Woman without a Shadow* because he thought it would stimulate an increase in the birth-rate. Strauss also went to London with the Dresden State Opera. He composed as well. But when he was seen among the audience at the Salzburg Festival after it had been announced that he had retired on grounds of ill health, many people began to realise that they had been misinformed, and most understood the reason why.

By the time of the Olympic Games in Berlin in 1936, Strauss had been partially rehabilitated in Nazi grace for his 'good behaviour'. This was essential now, because he had already composed the *Olympic Hymn*, a formal commission from the Committee of the Games. His conducting of it can be heard on the soundtrack of Part I of Lotte Riefenstahl's amazing film of the Games (given much public coverage before the 1972 German Olympics). Strauss asked for no royalties on this work, which is in any case a long way from his best; and when there was a collection in Garmisch by local representatives of the Games Committee, early in 1936, Frau Strauss refused to contribute and shooed them away with the words: 'He composed the damn thing for nothing, what more do you expect?'

Strauss was once again without a librettist since the loss of Zweig, who had fled abroad, and he was obliged to turn to a new one, Joseph Gregor. In his book about Strauss, published in 1939, Gregor wrote a short chapter on *The Silent Woman*, politely denigrating it, and managing to avoid a single reference to Zweig. But in 1937 he was cock-a-hoop at becoming the librettist to Germany's most important composer. For a long time, all his ideas for new subjects were tossed back at him by Strauss until one sunny afternoon, possibly out of depression and weariness at the situation in which he now found himself, Strauss accepted three librettos straight off. Gregor boasted that 'Four years' work were settled in a quarter of an hour!' One doubts that Strauss would seriously have taken such a short time to make such an important decision; the first opera, to be called *Friedenstag* ('Day of Peace') was already in progress between Zweig and Strauss, and Zweig—who had recommended Gregor—was on call whenever he might be needed. His concern for Strauss was touching and a silent refutation of those who charge the composer with Nazism.

It is difficult to understand how an opera with the message proclaimed by *Friedenstag* came to the stage in 1938, when the Nazis were poised for their assault on Poland in the following year, and were exultant over their invasion of Czechoslovakia. It tells of a beleaguered garrison during the Thirty Years War in which a fanatical Commander, who has never known peace, decides to blow up the citadel rather than submit. (In 1945, this is exactly what Hitler was and did.) When bells sound to signify the signing of Peace, he is dissuaded from this intention by his wife, Maria, and is persuaded to meet and to shake hands with his former enemy. The work ends with a paean of joy for peace among mankind.

Goebbels and a posse of Bavarian Nazi officials attended the first night in Munich. Strauss's supporters were understandably nervous, especially Clemens Krauss the conductor.

It might so easily go the wrong way and be banned like Strauss's preceding opera had been, and who else might be stigmatized this time? The cast were also feeling more squeamish than ordinary first night nerves can have stimulated. The only person who was in perfect command of himself as he stepped into the management box and sat down, was Richard Strauss.

As things turned out, the opera was accepted and received about one hundred performances in Germany and in Italy during the next two years; yet how it can have been accepted as representative of Nazi Germany in these years, is still a mystery. The opera is an enigma too, as its final situation can have several interpretations; the central character of the Commandant is left high and dry at the end with far more need for explanation and exposition than at the start. We simply don't know what happened to him.

With the successful launching of *Friedenstag*, Gregor's and Strauss's next opera *Daphne*, 'A bucolic tragedy' came out in Dresden three months later in a double bill with *Friedenstag*, the original intention. No politics beset this delightful work in which Strauss resorts to the (for him) unusual expedient of two principal tenors, one the shepherd Leukippos, and the other Apollo. The story tells of the nymph Daphne's pursuit by Leukippos, who adopts female clothing in order to get his way with her, which he nearly does. The god Apollo is so jealous that he destroys the shepherd with a thunderbolt but Daphne no longer wishes to remain human and is transmuted into a laurel tree. The opera is skilfully based on a half dozen themes which are woven and rewoven together to produce a feeling of such identity in the listener together with an atmosphere of great serenity and relaxation in the peacefully idyllic world of Greek shepherds and shepherdesses at the dawn of civilization. The pellucid texture of Strauss's score often belies the fact that he is using a fair sized orchestra.

Strauss and Gregor again sought Greek ideas for their next opera, a 'cheerful mythology in three acts', which was the third of the libretti which Strauss had so readily accepted from Gregor. It is called *Die Liebe der Danae*, 'The Love of Danae', and arose out of a combination of two legends: the visitation of Jupiter in a shower of golden rain, and Midas with the golden touch, and both directed at Danae. It seems rather a coincidence that Hofmannsthal had not only arrived at the same conjunction of legends himself, several years before, but that his sketch of it had been published in 1933. Gregor strenuously denied that he had set eyes on it. But when he and Strauss began to thrash out their libretto, Strauss was grateful for Hofmannsthal's sketch, as it contained a number of felicities which had altogether eluded Gregor. He also liked the lighter aspects of Hofmannsthal, as compared with Gregor's pomposities. Strauss completed the scoring of *Danae* at the end of June 1940, by which time the Nazi's hopes of conquering Britain were fading. No one in Germany had expected the war to last longer than the Spring of 1940, and Strauss was already anticipating the kind of change in public attitude which had happened between 1914 and 1918, and which he remembered only too well in connection with *The Woman without a Shadow*. He insisted that *Danae* must not be performed until at least two years after the war was over, when he expected not to be alive anyhow. Clemens Krauss eventually persuaded Strauss to change his mind, and *The Love of Danae* was scheduled to be the chief attraction at the abbreviated Salzburg Festival of 1944. Strauss was by now 80 years old and felt his age. He

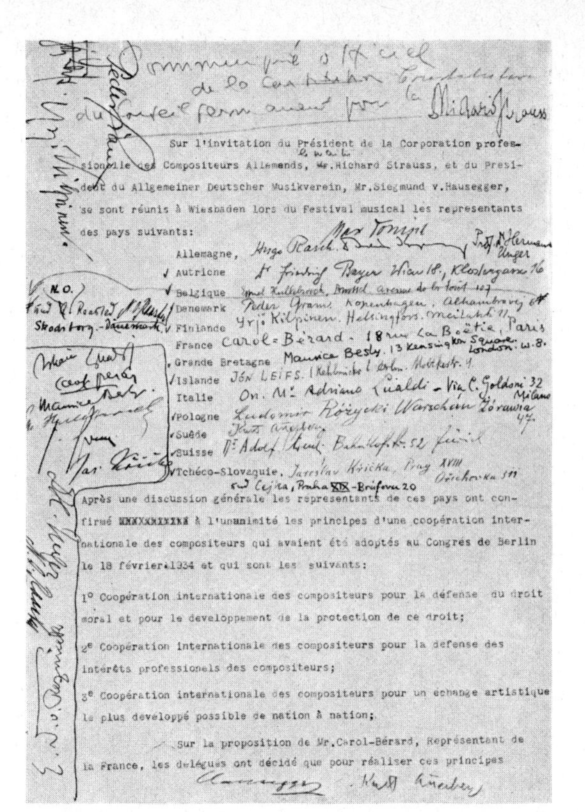

Sur l'invitation du Président de la Corporation professionelle des Compositeurs Allemands, Mr. Richard Strauss, et du President du Allgemeiner Deutscher Musikverein, Mr. Siegmund v. Hausegger, se sont réunis à Wiesbaden lors du Festival musical les representants des pays suivants:

Allemagne, Hugo Rasch ... Prof. Dr Hermann Unger
Autriche Dr Friedrich Bayer Wien 18., Klostergasse 16
Belgique
Denemark Peder Gram. Kopenhagen
Finlande Yrjö Kilpinen. Helsingfors.
France Carol-Bérard - 18 rue La Boëtie, Paris
Grande Bretagne Maurice Besly. 13 Kensington Square. London. W.8.
Islande Jón Leifs.
Italie On. Mo Adriano Lualdi - Via C. Goldoni 32 Milano
Pologne Ludomir Różycki Warschau Żorawia 47.
Suède
Suisse
Tchéco-Slovaquie, Jaroslav Křička, Prag XVIII

Après une discussion générale les representants de ces pays ont confirmé à l'unanimité les principes d'une coopération internationale des compositeurs qui avaient été adoptés au Congrès de Berlin le 18 février 1934 et qui sont les suivants:

1° Coopération internationale des compositeurs pour la défense du droit moral et pour le developpement de la protection de ce droit;

2° Coopération internationale des compositeurs pour la defense des intérêts professionels des compositeurs;

3° Coopération internationale des compositeurs pour un échange artistique le plus developpé possible de nation à nation;

Sur la proposition de Mr. Carol-Bérard, Représentant de la France, les délégués ont décidé que pour réaliser ces principes

Left: The opening page for the meeting of thirteen international musical bodies, endeavouring to combine under the presidency of Strauss in an attempt to regularize matters of composers' copyright throughout Europe and Russia in 1934. This French version of the text shows a number of interesting signatures.

Below: The facade of the Vienna State Opera, scene of many of Strauss's musical activities, which was severely bombed during World War II. The outside has been rebuilt to resemble exactly the former building, although the inside has been radically altered. It was re-opened in 1955.

Friedenstag: *Hans Hotter as the Commandant and Viorica Ursuleac as Maria, his wife, in a scene from the première of the opera in Munich in 1938 at a time when its theme must have seemed curiously inappropriate to the regime.*

was easier to convince than before, and Krauss was delighted at the chance of getting his hands on another new opera. In July 1944 there was an attempt on Hitler's life, known as the Generals' Plot, as a result of which there was intensive mobilization and cancellation of the Festival. Only Bayreuth survived the embargo on artistic enterprises. Owing to breakdown in communications, and thanks to the indulgence of Dr Scheel, the Gauleiter of Salzburg, *Danae* was allowed to proceed as far as the Dress Rehearsal, but no further. Thus Strauss saw performances of every one of his finished operas, and this occasion, though technically a rehearsal, was performed before an audience, and should count as the première rather than the official one eight years later.

Strauss was in a strangely unhappy mood. At an earlier rehearsal he had stood by the orchestra rail during the playing of one of the interludes, where he seemed to want to get as near to the music as he could. He waved to the musicians and said 'Perhaps we'll meet again in a better world!' After the performance was over he was discovered alone in a dressing room with the score of *Danae* in his hand, forecasting his impending departure from the earth and suggesting that the gods might let him take the score with him. But he soon shook himself out of this gloomy frame of mind, saying that his life's work was over, now that all the theatres in the Reich had been closed. He wrote a very lucid letter to Rudolf Hartmann, the producer of *Danae*, making suggestions and discussing the production.

As restrictions in Germany became more severe, due to the reversals which their army and air force were suffering, and as one opera house after another was bombed by the Allies, so Strauss seemed to shrink inside his large frame. Fortunately he had two influential allies, Baldur von Schirach and Reichsminister Dr Hans Frank. To the latter Strauss inscribed a personal message of thanks with a line of music—a thing he had for long liked to do as a token of gratitude to people who had helped or pleased him—but now to a person who was an out and out Nazi thug. This was for his help against Martin Bormann in preventing wounded Germans from being billeted on him. Strauss had said that he never wanted the War, and if it had not happened there would have been no wounded soldiers in any case. Strauss's daughter-in-law and his two grandsons dared no longer go outside for fear of being beaten up by local party members and ruffians. In any case they had for some time been prevented from shopping in 'Aryan' shops. Strauss was spied upon and reports were written about the undesirable company he kept, which made things more difficult for him at the time, but came in useful after the War as positive evidence in his favour.

Despite medical advice and recommendation, Strauss was not allowed to go abroad, and especially to Switzerland for cures and treatment. This probably hastened his death, for as well as urinary complaints, he had appendicitis at the age of 84, and all brought about by lack of correct diet and medical treatment.

On 30 April 1945 the first American arrived in Garmisch. When he walked up to Strauss's front door, the aged composer came out and said 'I am Dr Richard Strauss, the composer of *Der Rosenkavalier*!' This was reported to the senior officer, a Major Hayl, who saw to it that Strauss was given every assistance and civility. As soon as possible he and Pauline were put into a car and driven to the American-French border, since they had to travel through a French occupied zone in order to get to Switzerland. No one knew how the French would react, but they were equally helpful, and to demonstrate his gratitude and relief, Strauss gave the frontier commander a full score of *Der Alpensinfonie* in manuscript, which is now in the French National Library.

While he was in Switzerland, Strauss was called to attend a denazification court. As a former officer of the Music Chamber, he was automatically classed as Grade I—Guilty. But as before, when the Nazis had come to power and he had refused to take anything seriously, so he now ignored the command and stayed where he was. Strauss was exonerated and reinstated as a German citizen in June 1948, which could not be said for Clemens Krauss, Wilhelm Furtwängler and Baldur von Schirach. Krauss, on account of his efforts on behalf of the Third Reich and Furtwängler because of his having been a *Staatsrat* and an eventual fellow-traveller both languished until the end of 1949 as personae non grata. While they were both accepted into England as early as 1947, Furtwängler was not invited back to America. Baldur von Schirach, the Gauleiter of Vienna had been sympathetic to Strauss and had made it easier for the composer's 80th birthday celebrations in Vienna to go ahead. He also invited a chamber group to his house in the city where the first performance of the Sextet Introduction to the opera *Capriccio* was heard. Even so, these factors scarcely mitigated against his other misdeeds, and he was the last Nazi prisoner of high rank to remain in Spandau Prison, from which he was not released until 1970.

Strauss may be said to have come off very badly indeed from the two wars in which he was little more than a bystander. In the first instance he lost a fortune and was forced to alter radically the plans he had made for his future once he had reached the age of 50. At the end of the Second War he had lost a great deal more money and also his international reputation as a man. Even today, Israel still refuses to allow a note of his music to be played there. Toscanini is credited with having coined the salute: 'To Strauss the musician I take off my hat; to Strauss the man I put it on again.'

When he died in 1949, Strauss quite seriously thought that his music would not be played very much again, and nothing like the way in which it had been played over the past 40 years. He was completely wrong. Thanks to the far easier availability of music in the post-war years, by means of the long-playing gramophone record, television and tape recorders, Strauss's estate receives far more per annum today than he would have thought possible. The desperate old man who copied out full scores of his tone poems (usually from memory) either as a deposit against his inability to pay Swiss hoteliers, or else as an insurance policy for his grandsons against inflation, did the only thing he could—it was also the wisest thing he could. Thanks to the immense popularity of his music, Strauss's autograph scores are now worth far more than anyone but a millionaire can afford to pay.

Strauss's middle period, of influence and importance in German music, started soon after the Berne International Convention on copyright had been ratified. Not every country in the civilized world was a signatory, and within twelve years of this event Strauss began a struggle to try and free his fellow composers from a great deal of piracy on the part of music publishers. In 1898 Strauss and two other men—one a lawyer and musician called Friedrich Rösch—founded the German Society of Composers (GDT). Rösch wrestled with the legal side while Strauss did his best to gain support from his composing colleagues. At first they were wary of his intentions, but when they saw the draft proposals which he and Rösch put up before the Reichstag, many of the more influential ones joined in the struggle. Music publishers were nothing better than profiteers, paying a meagre once-and-for-all payment to composers for compositions, which were then completely out of their creators' control. The example which Strauss used to stress was Schubert, dying of starvation in Vienna, while a century later his publishers were making a fortune out of a cruel travesty of his inspiration called 'Lilac Time'. No longer must music be used contrary to the composers' intentions, and a proper copyright law should be passed.

Strauss lost the first round in the Reichstag where he and Rösch were up against an eloquent orator. So Strauss got to work and offered his own financial support, by way of expected future royalties, to the foundation of the Performing Rights Society (AFMA) in 1903. It worked in conjunction with the GDT. in the collection, administration and payment of royalties to composers. *Parsifal* had always been a very special opera to Strauss and in 1912

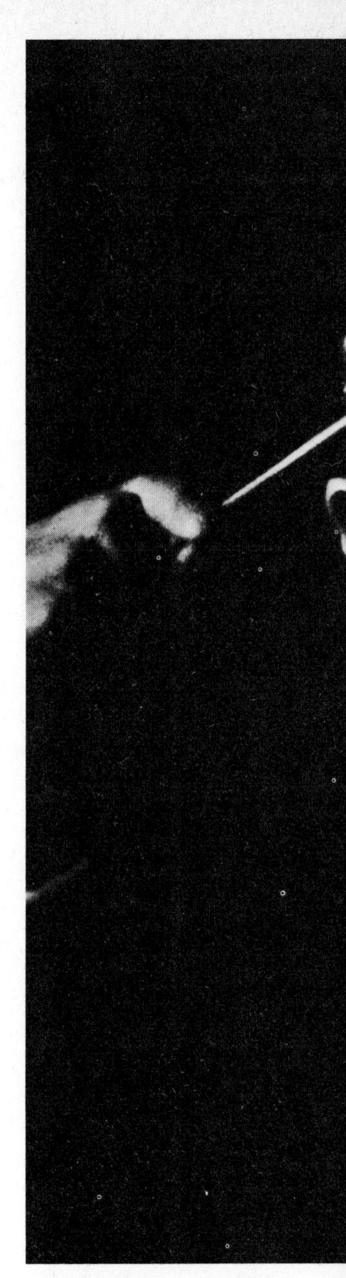

Strauss as the musicians saw him: confident, immovable, all-wise and never for a moment relaxing his control.

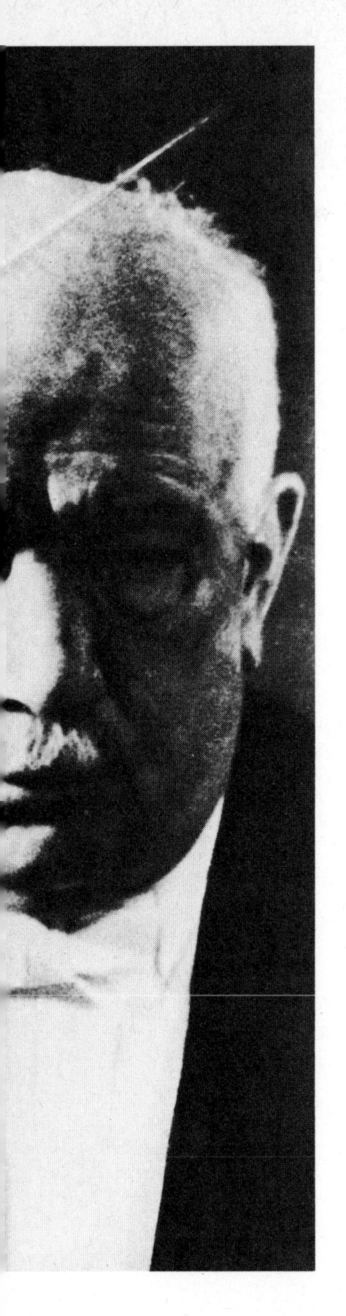

he wrote a very strong letter in connection with a questionnaire about the matter. He felt, as many Germans did—and still do—that Wagner's wishes concerning the opera should have been upheld: that it should be performed only at Bayreuth and as an act of artistic homage.

In 1915 the GEMA, a far better constituted version of the AFMA was founded, and more able to support the current move by the GDT to obtain a 50-year copyright law for German composers. But this was not forthcoming, although the Society was gaining much ground. All they obtained was this facility for 30 years. After the 1928 International Copyright Conference in Rome, at which no German government official attempted to do anything in the interest of his national composers, Strauss decided to take the law into his own hands as soon as the situation arose.

By now Rösch had died—prematurely. At his grave, Strauss gave a most moving oration which consisted of these words: 'Friedrich Rösch wrestled with the legislators for the rights of the German composer, and it is to him that the latter owes his dignity and independence of the publisher. . . . He dedicated all his energies, his fortune, his health and his life to his work.' This was in 1925.

In 1933 Strauss was made President of the Music Chamber, an office which seems to be appropriate in the context of his former years of endeavour in this direction. But of course it was a Nazi post. In the summer of 1934, Strauss's moment for a quick and last blow at the common enemy of music publishers came about. He was conducting Parsifal at Bayreuth and Hitler was there. He sought out Strauss and asked whether there was anything which, in a professional capacity, he needed. Strauss asked for:

a) 50 years protection by copyright in Germany
b) legal guarantee that *Parsifal* should be performed only at Bayreuth as Wagner wished
c) protection against inartistic and irrelevant arrangements of serious compositions.

Hitler was impressed and told Goebbels to look into it. But the Minister of Propaganda did not agree with the Führer for he at once devised a scheme whereby monies gained by an extension of the copyright period from 30 to 50 years would go into a special fund that he would set up at the Ministry of Propaganda. The Bavarian Minister of Justice, Hofrat Frank, saw a way out of it all that did not publicly set Goebbels against Hitler, a fact that left Frank very much in Strauss's debt. What they achieved was the complete 50 year copyright period for composers as in any other Berne Convention country, as well as proper protection against unnecessary and inartistic arrangements. But Bayreuth did not succeed in getting its monopoly of *Parsifal*. Strauss's part in the stabilizing of German composers' rights and the preservation of a minimum reward for their labours can thus be seen to have been of crucial and long term importance.

Musical politics were also centred, in Strauss's life, round Salzburg. There had been small festivals there since 1861, but even during the First World War, Strauss, Hofmannsthal and Max Reinhardt discussed ways and means of promoting a large-scale annual music and drama festival there. The fact that all this was being negotiated during hostilities, shows the far-sightedness—not so much of Strauss to whom the War was of no consequence—but of the others. The first Festival consisted of some performances of Hofmannsthal's 'Everyman' (*Jedermann*) in 1920. The production was by Reinhardt, and elements of this early production still survive in re-presentations of the morality play in the Domplatz today. In 1921 this experiment was repeated with success, and in 1922, the first operas were given. Strauss conducted the first: *Don Giovanni*. And from then and until 1933, when he conducted some memorable performances of *Fidelio*, Strauss was frequently to be found on the podium of the Festspielhaus. The Nazis forced him out, and although he conducted two concerts there afterwards, he never again appeared in the opera pit. Salzburg was the first of the twentieth century style of international music festivals, and (Bayreuth apart, which is not international at all but very parochial in outlook) has remained by far the most successful. It was at Salzburg too where Strauss witnessed his last première, of *Die Liebe der Danae*, 22 years to the day after he had first lifted his baton there and begun the stream of Festival music in the town of Mozart's birth.

Chapter 8

Strauss's Late Spring

Like Verdi, who astonished the world with his last opera *Falstaff*, Strauss produced in the extremity of his age a group of works which are not simply remarkable for their complete mastery of their subjects but which seem to sparkle with a new-found youth. These are so numerous in fact that they merit a chapter to themselves.

As he grew older, Strauss was more inclined to the reflective and tranquil in music, paring down his great orchestral colourings of years gone by from the tone poems to the *Alpensinfonie* and *The Woman without a Shadow*, so that they became more classical in weight as well as in structure. In some cases they were tinged with an immense sadness, for many of the good things of his long life were disappearing round him.

Strauss's late spring can be said to have begun with the deft gossamer fabric of *Daphne*, which expresses his longing for the golden era of mythological, classical Greece where, at times, he felt he truly belonged. Likewise, with *The Love of Danae*, in which he almost saw himself as Jupiter, old Strauss returned to the Greece he loved, to justify his place on Mount Olympus. The last composition in this pseudo-Grecian manner is a pendant to *Daphne*. It is an unused choral finale to the opera which Strauss altered, added a line for boys, and tailored to suit the Vienna State Opera Chorus Concerts with their famous boy singers.

Daphne and the words of the Chorale 'To the Daphne Tree' were, of course, written by Joseph Gregor. After the completion of the text of *Danae*, Gregor was looking forward to working with Strauss on the next opera, later to be called *Capriccio*. But Strauss had had quite enough of Gregor, though he kept him on a string for as long as he lived, in case he might come in useful. He treated Gregor cavalierly, and openly wrote to him that he was hearily sick of the word *Geliebter*! ('Beloved!) with which he liberally sprinkled all his libretti. Had Gregor had any kind of *amour propre* he would have left Strauss; but he was apparently unmoved by insults and popped up again as if nothing had happened. *Capriccio* may be said to have had six librettists, in that ideas for the text were contributed by Hofmannsthal long before; by Stefan Zweig who set the germinating ideas in motion; by Joseph Gregor who took them up; by Clemens Krauss who took them over; by Hans Swarossky who contributed the translation of the Sonnet and several other moments in the text; and finally by Strauss himself who, when he had abandoned Gregor altogether, became joint librettist with Krauss and Swarowsky. But Krauss got his way over dropping Swarowsky's name as joint author.

Although *Capriccio* was written and composed after *Danae*, it was staged before it, in 1942 in Munich, where the admirable team of Krauss, Hartmann and Sievert (as conductor, producer and designer) were creating such new standards of opera production, especially in the field of Strauss's works, that Munich has since been to him what Bayreuth is to Wagner. *Capriccio* is an opera for opera lovers. It is also an opera within an opera for it tells of the endeavours of a widowed Countess—still young and very beautiful—to separate in her mind two young artists. They are a poet and a composer who both crave her love. Symbolizing as she does the Spirit of Opera, she is of course unable to be with one to the exclusion of the other; and when at the end of *Capriccio* she finds that she has made an assignation with them both at the same time and at the same place, she realises that poetry and music are indivisible in opera. Even so, the work ends with a question. She has to choose one but how can she? Opposed to the Countess, the Poet and the Composer is an old theatre director

(based on Max Reinhardt it is said) called La Roche, whose ideas of opera are definitely outdated. The setting of *Capriccio* is round about 1770, at the time of Gluck's operatic reforms, and a highly significant time for the art, which was about to be entirely revitalized and given new direction. So the many-sided *Capriccio* tells a variety of stories through parables and imaginative expression, which is the whole clue to the purpose of the opera. To listen to it on the surface of the story is to miss a great deal. The musical core of the first part of the work (which is in one continuous act) is a sonnet, first spoken by the Count (Countess Madeleine's brother) and his mistress to be, the actress Clairon. The sonnet is by the sixteenth-century poet, Ronsard, though in the opera it has ostensibly been written by the Poet. Its setting by the Composer in the opera, as a trio by the two men and the Countess is very effective. Later on the Count introduces a melody to the words 'Opera is the absurdest thing!' This melody is none other than the glorious piano rhapsody which comes into No's 8 and 12 in the *Krämerspiegel* set of 12 songs that Strauss wrote in 1918 as his musical diatribe against greedy publishers. Strauss used it to mark a moonlight scene indelibly on the memories of all those who have seen the opera staged.

Strauss was present at the rehearsals of *Capriccio* and was certain that this was going to be his last opera première, for his ban on *Danae* was still in operation. He decided that the most appropriate way of finishing his life's work in opera was in the key of D♭. 'What better key?' he asked, for this is the key in which he wrote many of his purple passages: the trio in *Der Rosenkavalier*, the love duet between Ariadne and Bacchus, the Grundlsee Waltz in *Intermezzo*, and so on. Yet even this was not to be his last opera project, not quite, for, after several false starts, he and Gregor set to work on another Greek tale. It was never finished, so need not concern us unduly, and merely shows that a Strauss work completed by another hand is nothing like Strauss at all. 'The Donkey's Shadow', as it is called, was for the boys of the Ettal Monastery School, where Strauss's son and one of his grandsons had been educated.

Perhaps the most telling works of this golden late spring are those for orchestra. There is the *Divertimento*, an extended version of the ballet *Verklungene Feste* that Strauss made out of pieces by Couperin. There are also three concertos for small orchestra, one for oboe, one for horn and a rare one for solo clarinet and bassoon, the *Duo Concertino*. The oboe concerto was recorded by Léon Goossens in London at the end of 1947, and is now one of the most difficult yet delicious showpieces in the oboe repertoire. Goossens' recording embodies a finale which Strauss decided to alter afterwards, yet before the score had gone to the engraver. The *Duo Concertino* came as easily to Strauss, and there is no 'note-spinning' here at all. In fact Strauss in these last years had stopped 'note-spinning' altogether: everything he was to compose from now onwards had the pure spark of genius. He uses a string orchestra to accompany the two woodwind instruments, but with the interesting addition of a harp.

Above: After the première of Capriccio *in 1924, Strauss with (left) Hildegard Ranczak and (behind him) his son Franz Strauss.*

Previous page: Strauss pauses in rehearsal to make a point to the leader, who is sitting just below the point from which this photograph was taken.

Above: A touching picture of Strauss towards the end of his life, a refugee in Switzerland: miserably poor, cold and hungry and without any hope for the future. Had the Nazis allowed him into Switzerland earlier for necessary operations, had he lived a few years longer, he would have seen and heard how his life's work began to blossom again and to occupy a permanent and much loved place in the world's musical heritage.

Bust of Strauss by Hugo Lederer.

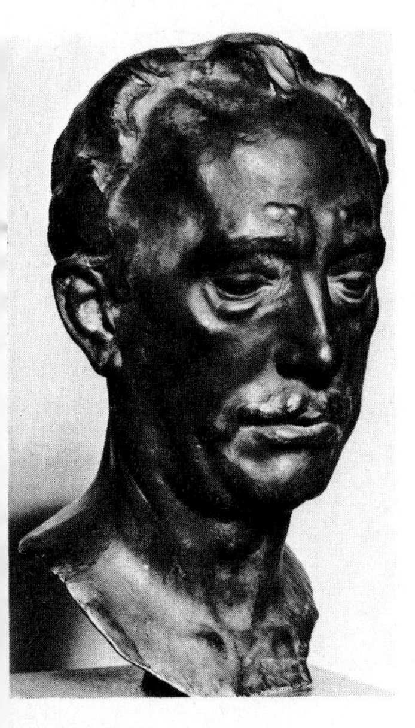

This was certainly a pleasant exercise for Strauss in sharpening his musical faculties even at the advanced age of 83. But of these three concertos, it is probably the second horn concerto which is best known. It is in a fairly conventional mould, with a hunting rondo as the last movement; a jovial, masculine piece, in which the horn again demands to be heard solo at the outset. I say 'again' because in Strauss's first horn concerto, Opus 11, he had done the same striking thing in 1883, almost 60 years back.

Strauss now ventured into still smaller compositions, more or less chamber music, for sixteen instruments. Between 1942 and 1945 he composed two Sonatinas, the first (in F) in three movements, and the second (in E♭) in four. The second, which is the better of the two is dedicated 'To the divine Mozart at the end of a life filled with gratitude'.

Contrasted with all these fresh and youthfully inclined works are two of vastly different mood. They are firstly a 'Study for 23 solo strings' called *Metamorphosen*, and an orchestral piece called *München*—'A Memorial Waltz'. In March 1945, when most Germans must have been looking over their shoulders at the possibility of defeat, Strauss wrote to Gregor in the very nadir of depression. 'Goethe's house, the world's greatest holy place destroyed! My lovely Dresden, Weimar, Munich, all gone!' Ten days later the Vienna State Opera suffered the same fate. Every opera house in which Strauss had lived and worked and enjoyed his greatest successes were now heaps of rubble. It was as if everything he had attempted to achieve in a long life-long devotion to music had been symbolically destroyed within a few months.

After the First War's greatest blows Strauss found consolation in hard work. Again he turned to his desk and composed two memorials to the appalling desolation. *Metamorphosen* is a long and beautiful dirge, based on Beethoven's Funeral March in the slow movement of the 'Eroica' Symphony. It is a work of such expanse and poignancy that it breathes the very soul of sadness.

In 1939 Strauss had composed a jolly and 'occasional' Waltz called 'Munich' which was intended for a film about the city that never materialized. This version of the Waltz is in manuscript and has never been heard, although the manuscript is in the Bavarian State Library. Now Strauss took the Waltz as a basis for his threnody on the destruction of Munich, his beautiful birth-place, and added an alarming centre section which is indeed very bitter. Prophetically the work reverts to its happy start again, constructed as it is in three sections.

After all this there was still something left to come. It was to be perhaps the finest distillation of the old and resigned Strauss, with a lifetime of writing for the voice, and especially the soprano voice, behind him. This was the set of four songs, although there was a sketch for a fifth on his desk when he got up from it for the last time. The four which he completed, for soprano and full orchestra, have come to be known as the 'Four Last Songs'. Strauss may have been intending to write a group, either of four or five, or more, we shall never know. The four songs he completed were first performed in London in May 1950 by Kirsten Flagstad and the Philharmonia Orchestra under Wilhelm Furtwängler, and later rearranged in a different order to make a kind of song-cycle: *Frühling* (Spring); *September*; *Beim Schlafengehen* (Going to Sleep) and *Im Abendrot* (Sunset). Flagstad's voice was not ideal for this kind of vocal melisma, but she and Furtwängler happened to be in London together. It was Lisa Della Casa and later still Elisabeth Schwarzkopf who made Strauss's Four Last Songs familiar to thousands of people.

Strauss took to his bed for the last time at the end of August 1949, following a series of heart attacks and increased urinary trouble. The producer, Rudolf Hartmann, was one of only a very few people who were welcome, others being Karl Böhm and Willi Schuh, though they were not nearby. Hartmann gives a vivid account of his last visit to the dying composer. Strauss said: 'Good that you are here. Sit down beside me.' And then he went on: 'Death has dealt me the first hard blow, it has given me the first sign.' Then he went on to talk very sensibly and with great fervour about the need for re-birth of the Theatre in Europe. 'So many things for me still to do—but I think that some of the things that I intended and which I started off, have fallen on fruitful ground.' He went on to express his sorrow at the loss of so many German theatres, and gave his views as to who should be put into the key artistic positions for rebuilding them;

he also considered the various futures of the opera houses still left standing. Then with a smile he said to Hartmann 'We would have divided the world rather well—our world!' Then, rather surprisingly he said: '*Gruss mir die Welt*' (Greet the world for me), and asked 'Where does that come from?' Hartmann suggested *Die Walküre* but Strauss shook his head. 'No, no, it's not that, these words come from somewhere else'. They in fact come from Act I of *Tristan und Isolde* but Strauss never remembered, for after a long silence he looked so tired that Hartmann decided that it was time to leave. Richard Strauss grasped his hand and said 'Perhaps we'll see each other again; if not, then you know everything.' And with a sob he turned away as Hartmann left the room. A day or two later, Strauss observed to his daughter-in-law 'It's a funny thing, Alice, dying is just how I composed it in *Tod und Verklärung*!' These are his last reported words, for on 8 September 1949, Richard Strauss died. He was cremated in Munich four days later. At his special request, the trio from *Der Rosenkavalier* was sung at the service.

Strauss left behind him a Testament which gives an idea of how he saw a rebirth of Opera in Germany. He envisaged each city where there was an opera house having, in fact two houses, one called the Opera Museum, and the other the Opera Playhouse. The repertoire for the Play House is too long to give complete, but all Strauss's operas were included and everything by Wagner from an uncut *Rienzi* to *Gotterdämmerung*. Strauss evidently considered that *Parsifal* should remain sacrosanct to Bayreuth. Verdi's *Aïda*, *Simone Boccanegra* and *Falstaff* were the three he chose for the Opera Museum, but of the rest there were to be none of the early operas, 'because as complete works they are unbearable for us today'. Instead, he visualized a potpourri of scenes from them. As for Verdi's *Otello*, he wrote 'I condemn it altogether, as I do all opera texts which spoil the classic plays, as for example, Gounod's *Faust*, Rossini's *William Tell* and Verdi's *Don Carlos*. They do not belong to the German stage.'

Strauss wrote out his Will and sent two copies (very slightly different) to Karl Böhm by different posts, in case one was destroyed, or he, Strauss, did not survive the War. He did survive it all, and even went to several performances of opera in Munich; he was planning and thinking and making himself feel part of the post-war opera scene right until the end of his life.

Nowhere is there exactly the kind of organization which he prescribed, and nowhere is there the same direction or accent upon the groups of operas which he considered were the best for the German theatre. This is because he overlooked or was unable to grasp the fact that there were going to be immense changes in habits and outlook in Germany and in Europe, that the younger people would want something—and would get something—entirely different, and that not so long after his death, prominent musicians would be preaching in thin voices that opera is a dead art, that far from there being the need for a 'museum of opera', the whole thing should be consigned to the scrap-heap.

Fortunately this has not happened—not yet—despite this desire in the minds of such operatic Jeremiahs as Pierre Boulez, who nevertheless conducts it with apparent conviction, albeit with some originality. So far as Strauss's operas are concerned, they are given greater currency than ever before, save by M. Boulez, who has publicly stated that he will never, under any circumstances, conduct any music by Tchaikovsky, Puccini or Richard Strauss. Yet these three composers' popularity is swelling every season because of the immense love of and need for their music.

Strauss once said of himself that he knew he was not a first-rate composer, but he reckoned himself to be a 'first-class second-rate' composer and this perhaps sums it all up better than anybody else might think. It has also been said that genius is 1% inspiration and 99% perspiration. Strauss was used to hard work. As we know his whole life was geared to producing the results of it. And this accounts for the first-class part. It was only the elusive 1% of genius which sometimes was there—sometimes was not. But then—he knew.

No man, be he artist or not, can ask more than to know himself and his own capabilities and few men achieve it. Strauss was one of the rare ones. For we who come after there is the magnificent body of works to lead us to an understanding of this complex and brilliantly talented man. Between *Don Juan* of 1889 and *September* of 1948 lie all the clues: his music tells us everything.

Above; Dr Karl Böhm conducting the Berlin Philharmonic Orchestra in the performance of a Strauss symphonic poem.

Main Events in Strauss's Life

1864 Richard Georg Strauss born at 6 am on 11 June at Altheimer Eck 2, Munich.
1867 His sister Johanna born 9 June.
1868 Starts piano lessons with August Tombo (Court Harpist).
1871 First compositions: Christmas Song and Tailor's Polka.
First visits to the opera in Munich.
1872 Starts violin lessons with Benno Walter.
1874–82 Attends Royal Ludwigsgymnasium in Munich.
1875 Starts lessons in theory and composition with F. W. Meyer.
1881 First composition published: *Festmarsch* Op. 1.
1882–83 Attends Munich University: philosophy, aesthetics, history of art.
First visit to Bayreuth with his father.
1883–84 Visits Dresden, Berlin and Leipzig.
1884 First meeting with Bülow. Summer in Feldafing.
Conducts his Wind Serenade in Munich.
1885 Accepts conducting post under Bülow at Meiningen.
After one month is in sole charge there. Meets Brahms.
1886 Leaves Meiningen. First visit to Italy.
Hears *Tristan* and *Parsifal* at Bayreuth.
Becomes third conductor at Munich Court Opera.
1887 Meets Pauline de Ahna at Feldafing and Mahler in Leipzig.
1889 Musical Assistant at Bayreuth for *Parsifal*.
Leaves Munich and becomes second conductor at Weimar.
Don Juan given there: a great success.
1890 Guest conductor of the Berlin Philharmonic Orchestra.
1891 Falls ill with pleurisy and pneumonia during the summer.
Spends Christmas with Cosima Wagner at Bayreuth.
1892 Conducts *Tristan* at Weimar.
Second illness with severe pleurisy and bronchitis.
Goes to Greece, Egypt and Italy to convalesce.
Works on *Guntram*.
1894 Leaves Weimar. Marries Pauline de Ahna.
Court Conductor in Munich. Berlin Philharmonic Symphony Concerts conductor owing to the death of Bülow.
1896 Becomes principal conductor in Munich.
Starts series of European conducting tours.
1897 Son Franz born on 12 April.
1898 Leaves Munich and becomes Conductor at Berlin Court Opera.
Takes up residence in Berlin.
1899 First meets Rolland in Berlin. First visit to England.
1900 First meets Hofmannsthal in Paris.
1901 Becomes Chairman of *ADMV* (until 1909).
First première at Dresden Opera with *Feuersnot*.
1903 Foundation of *AFMA*. Gains Ph.D. from Heidelberg.
1904 First concert tour to USA with his wife.
1905 Death of father, Franz Strauss, 31 May.
Salome performed in Dresden on 9 December.
1908 Garmisch villa is finished.
General Music Director at Berlin Court Opera (until 1918).
1909 *Elektra* in Dresden on 25 January.
Is succeeded as Chairman of the *ADMA* by Schillings.
1910 Death of his mother on 16 May.
Is created Knight of the Order of Maximilian.
1911 *Rosenkavalier* in Dresden on 25 January.
1912 'Bourgeois' *Ariadne* at Stuttgart on 25 October.
1914 *Josephslegende* in Paris and London. Made Hon.D.Mus. (Oxon).
50th birthday plaque placed on his birthplace in Munich.
Fortune confiscated by Bank of England on outbreak of War.
1917 Co-founder of Salzburg Festival Association.
Conducts the 100th Dresden *Rosenkavalier* on 13 December.
1918 Leaves Berlin Court Opera. Returns as Intendant (for one year) of Berlin State Opera.
1919 Becomes co-director of Vienna State Opera with Franz Schalk.
Frau ohne Schatten in Vienna on 10 October.
1920 Leaves Berlin Statskappelle (formerly Court Orchestra) and is succeeded by Furtwängler.
1922 Publication of Correspondence with Hofmannsthal (abridged).
1924 Marriage of son Franz Strauss with Alice Grab in Vienna on 15 January. Many awards and honours for 60th birthday Leaves Vienna State Opera and last permanent post.
1926 Reconciled with Vienna State Opera and returns to conduct from time to time.
1927 Grandson Richard Strauss born on 1 November.
1929 Death of Hofmannsthal on 15 July
1933 Conducts *Parsifal* for Toscanini at Bayreuth on 1 July.
Made President of Reich's Music Chamber. *Arabella* in Dresden.
1934 Many ceremonies, awards and festivals for 70th Birthday.
1935 *Schweigsame Frau* in Dresden on 24 June. Rift with Nazi régime.
Relinquishes Presidency of Chamber of Music.
1936 Forbidden to conduct for one year in the Reich.
Conducts abroad, including London, where he receives Gold Medal of the Royal Philharmonic Society.
Composes Hymn for the Berlin Olympic Games.
1937 Partly re-established, politically.
Beginning of successful Krauss-Hartmann-Sievert productions of Strauss's operas in Munich.
1938 *Friedenstag* in Munich on 24 July; *Daphne* in Dresden on 15 October.
1942 *Capriccio* in Munich on 28 October. Health indifferent.
1944 80th Birthday celebrations. *Liebe der Danae* in Salzburg on 16 August. Golden Wedding 10 September.
1945 Utter misery at loss of opera houses. Artistic Testament to Böhm. Goes to Switzerland at end of War on 15 October.
1947 Flies to London for series of Strauss concerts.
1948 Severely ill in Lausanne.
1949 Returns to Garmisch on 10 May and dies there on 8 Sept.

Compositions

OPERAS

Guntram
In 3 Acts. Libretto by Strauss. 1887–93. Opus 25. WP Court Theatre Weimar, 10 May 1894 under Strauss.
Revised version National Theatre Weimar, 29 October, 1940 under Paul Sixt.
Not performed in Britain or in USA.

Feuersnot
'Sung Poem' in 1 Act. Libretto by Ernst von Wolzogen. 1900–01. Opus 50. WP Court Opera Dresden, 22 November 1901 under Ernst von Schuch.
Britain: His Majesty's Theatre London, 9 July 1910.
USA: Philadelphia (visit of Metropolitan Opera) 1 December 1927.

Salome
Drama in 1 Act. Libretto adapted by Strauss from Hedwig Lachmann's German translation of Oscar Wilde's play. 1903–05. Opus 54.
WP Court Opera Dresden, 9 December 1905 under Schuch.
Britain: Covent Garden, London, 8 December 1910.
USA: Metropolitan Opera, New York, 22 January 1907.

Elektra
Tragedy in 1 Act. Libretto by Hugo von Hofmannsthal. Opus 58. 1906–08.
WP Court Opera Dresden, 25 January 1910 under Schuch.
Britain: Covent Garden, London, 19 February 1910.

USA: Manhattan O.H., New York, 1 February 1910.

Der Rosenkavalier
Comedy for Music in 3 Acts. Libretto by Hofmannsthal. 1909–10. Opus 59. WP Court Opera Dresden, 26 January 1911 under Schuch.
Britain: Covent Garden, London 29 January 1913.
USA: Metropolitan Opera, New York, 9 December 1913.

Ariadne auf Naxos
in First Version as pendant to *Le Bourgeois Gentilhomme*, adaptation of Molière's play and opera libretto by Hofmannsthal.
Comedy with dances. 1911–12. Opus 60.
WP Stuttgart Court Theatre, 25 October 1912 under Strauss.
Britain: His Majesty's Theatre, 27 May 1913.
USA: Not performed
in Second Version, Prologue and Opera.
WP Vienna Court Opera, 4 October 1916, under Franz Schalk.
Britain: Covent Garden, London, 27 May 1924.
USA: Philadelphia, 1 November 1928.

Die Frau ohne Schatten
Opera in 3 Acts. Libretto by Hofmannsthal 1914–18. Opus 65. WP Vienna State Opera 10 October 1919 under Schalk.
Britain: Sadler's Wells Theatre, London, 2 May 1966 (Visit of Hamburg State Opera).
USA: San Francisco, 18 September 1959.

Intermezzo
A bourgeois comedy with symphonic interludes in 2 Acts. Libretto by Strauss. 1918–23. Opus 72. WP Dresden State Opera, 4 November 1924 under Fritz Busch.
Britain: King's Theatre, Edinburgh, 9 September 1965 (Visit of Bavarian State Opera to Edinburgh Festival).
USA: No stage performance.

Die ägyptische Helena
Opera in 2 Acts by Hugo von Hofmannsthal. 1924–27. Opus 75. WP Dresden State Opera 6 June 1928 under Fritz Busch.
Britain: Not performed.
USA: Metropolitan Opera, New York, 26 November 1928.
Revised 'Vienna' Version by Clemens Krauss 1st performed at Salzburg Festival Theatre on 14 August 1933 under Krauss.

Arabella
Lyrical comedy in 3 Acts by Hugo von Hofmannsthal. 1929–32. Opus 79. WP Dresden State Opera, 1 July 1933 under Krauss.
Britain: Covent Garden, London, 17 May 1934 (Visit of Dresden State Opera).
USA: Metropolitan Opera, New York, 10 February

Die schweigsame Frau
Comic Opera in 3 Acts. Freely adapted from Ben Jonson by Stefan Zweig. 1932–35. Opus 80. WP Dresden State Opera, 24 June 1935 under Karl Böhm.
Britain: Covent Garden, London, 20 November 1961.
USA: New York City Opera, 7 October 1958.

Friedenstag
Opera in 1 Act by Joseph Gregor. 1935–36. Opus 81. WP Munich National Theatre, 24 July 1938 under Krauss.
Britain: Not performed.
USA: Los Angeles 2 April 1967.

Daphne
Bucolic Tragedy in 1 Act by Joseph Gregor. 1936–37. Opus 82. WP Dresden State Opera 15 October 1938 under Böhm.
Britain: Not performed.
USA: No stage performance.

Die Liebe der Danae
'Cheerful Mythology' in 3 Acts by Joseph Gregor. 1938–40. WP as Public Dress Rehearsal for cancelled première at the Salzburg Festival Theatre, 16 August 1944 under Krauss; official WP at the Salzburg Festival Theatre, 14 August 1952 under Krauss.
Britain: Covent Garden, London 16 September 1953 under Rudolf Kempe (Visit of Bavarian State Opera).
USA: Los Angeles 5 April 1964.

Capriccio
A conversation piece for music in 1 Act by Clemens Krauss and Strauss. 1940–41. Opus 85. WP Munich State Opera (National Theatre) under Krauss, 28 October 1942.
Britain: Covent Garden, London 22 September 1953 under Robert Heger (Visit of Bavarian State Opera).
USA: Santa Fé, 1 August 1958.

Des Esels Schatten
Posthumous '*Singspiel*' (unfinished). Libretto by Hans Adler. 1947–49. No opus number. 1st performances on 7 and 14 June 1964 at the Ettal Monastery. 1st professional performance, Court Theatre of the Palace, Naples, under Franco Mannino.
Britain: St. Pancras Town Hall, London, 27 May 1970.

MUSIC FOR THE STAGE

Chorus from the Elektra of Sophocles
1880. No opus number. WP Munich, Ludwigsgymnasium in 1880.

Iphégénie en Tauride (Gluck)
New version, with added trio by Strauss. 1890. No opus number.
WP Weimar Court Theatre under Kryzonorski, 9 June 1900.

Festmusik
Accompaniment to tableaux vivants.
1892. No opus number. WP Weimar, Court Orchestra under Strauss, 8 October 1892.

Der Bürger als Edelmann
Comedy by Molière in free adaptation in German by Hugo von Hofmannsthal. Original incidental music extended. 1917. (Opus 60).
WP Berlin, Deutsches Theater, 9 April 1918.

Die Ruinen von Athen
A festival play with dances and choruses. Newly edited by Hugo von Hofmannsthal with music of Beethoven arranged, and with one melodramatic scene newly composed, by Strauss. 1924. No opus number.
WP Vienna State Opera under Strauss, 20 September 1924.

Idomeneo (Mozart)
Completely new arrangement by Strauss and Lothar Wallerstein, with new numbers composed by Strauss. 1930. No opus number. WP Vienna State Opera under Strauss, 16 April 1931.

BALLET MUSIC

Josephslegende
Action in one act by Harry Count Kessler and Hugo von Hofmannsthal

1912–14. Opus 63. WP Paris Opéra, Ballets Russes de Diaghilev, under Strauss, 14 May 1914.

Schlagobers
Gay Viennese Ballet in two acts by Strauss. 1921–22. Opus 70. WP Vienna State Opera under Strauss, 9 May 1924.

Tanzsuite after Couperin, for small orchestra
1922–23. No opus number. WP Vienna State Opera under Krauss, 17 February 1923.

Verklungene Feste
The Couperin *Tanzsuite* augmented by six additional numbers. 1940. No opus number. WP Munich State Opera under Krauss, 5 April 1941.

Divertimento. Verklungene Feste augmented by two further pieces. 1941. Opus 86. (Final version).

TONE POEMS

Macbeth
After Shakespeare's Drama for full orchestra. 1886–88. (Opus 23.)
1st version rejected and not publicly performed.
2nd version 1889–90. Opus 23. WP Weimar, Court Orchestra under Strauss, 13 October 1890.

Don Juan
After Nikolaus Lenau for full orchestra. 1887–89. Opus 20. WP Weimar, Court Orchestra under Strauss, 11 November 1889.

Tod und Verklärung
For full orchestra. 1888–89. Opus 24. WP Eisenach, Tonkünstlerfest under Strauss, 21 June 1890.

Till Eulenspiegels lustige Streiche
After the old rogue's tune—in Rondeau form—set for full orchestra. 1894–95. Opus 28. WP Cologne, City Orchestra under Franz Wüllner, 5 November 1895.

Also sprach Zarathustra
Freely after Friedrich Nietzsche for full orchestra. 1895–96. Opus 30. WP Frankfort on Main, City Orchestra under Strauss, 27 November 1896.

Don Quixote
Introduction, theme and variations and Finale. Fantastic variations on a theme of knightly character for full orchestra. 1897. Opus 35. WP Cologne, City Orchestra under Wüllner, 8 March 1898.

Ein Heldenleben
For full orchestra. 1897–98. Opus 40. WP Frankfort on Main, City Orchestra under Strauss, 3 March 1899.

SYMPHONIES

1st Symphony in D minor for full orchestra.
1880. No opus number. WP Munich Court Orchestra under Hermann Levi, 30 March 1881. (Manuscript).

2nd Symphony in F minor for full orchestra.
1883–84. Opus 12. WP New York, Philharmonic Orchestra under Theodor Thomas, 13 December 1884.

Sinfonia domestica in one movement for full orchestra.
1902–03. Opus 53. WP New York, Strauss Festival. Wetzler Symphony Orchestra under Strauss, 21 March 1904.

Eine Alpensinfonie in one movement for full orchestra and organ.
1911–15. Opus 64. WP Berlin, Dresden Court Orchestra under Strauss, 18 October 1915. There is also a reduced version without organ made in 1934.

'Symphony for Wind Instruments' see *2nd Sonatina for 16 Wind Instruments* on page 110.

CONCERTI AND WORKS FOR SOLO INSTRUMENT AND ORCHESTRA

Violin and Orchestra in D minor.
1881–82. Opus 8. WP with piano accompaniment only: Vienna, Benno Walter, Violin; Strauss, piano, 5 December 1882.

Horn and Orchestra No. 1 in E♭.
1882–83. Opus 11. WP Meiningen. Gustav Leinhos with the Meiningen Court Orchestra under Hans von Bülow, 4 March 1885.

Horn and Orchestra No. 2 in E♭.
1942. No opus number. WP Salzburg. Gottfried von Freiburg with the Vienna Philharmonic Orchestra under Karl Böhm, 11 August 1943.

Burleske for Piano and Orchestra (one movement)
1885–86. No opus number. WP Eisenach, Tonkunstlerfestorchester under Strauss with Eugen d'Albert, piano.

Parergon zur Sinfonia domestica for Piano (left hand) and Orchestra.
1924–25. Opus 73. Commissioned by Paul Wittgenstein and played by him at the WP in Dresden with the State Orchestra under Fritz Busch on 16 October 1925.

Panathenäenzug
Symphonic Studies in the form of a Passacaglia for piano (left hand) and orchestra. Opus 74. 1926–27. Commissioned by Paul Wittgenstein and played by him at the WP in Vienna, with the Vienna Philharmonic Orchestra under Franz Schalk on 11 March 1928.

Cadenzas to Mozart's Piano Concerto in C minor, K.491.
1885. No opus number. WP Meiningen, Strauss (piano) and the Meiningen Court Orchestra under Hans von Bülow.

Festliches Präludium for full orchestra and organ.
1913. Opus 61. Vienna, Konzerthaus (for its opening). Konzertverein Orchestra under Friedrich Löwe, 19 October 1913.

Oboe and small orchestra
1945–46. No opus number. WP Zürich, Marcel Saillet (oboe) with Tonhalle Orchestra under V. Andreae, 26 February 1946.

Duet Concertino for Clarinet, Bassoon and String Orchestra with Harp.
1947. No opus number. WP Lugano Radio with Armando Basile (clarinet), Bruno Bergamaschi (bassoon) and Orchestra della Radio Svizzera Italiana under O. Nussio, 4 April 1948.

OTHER ORCHESTRAL WORKS

1st Festmarsch in E♭.
1876. Opus 1. WP Munich, Wilde Gung'l Orchestra under Franz Strauss, 26 March 1881.

Aus Italien
Symphonic Fantasy in G for full orchestra. 1886. Opus 16. WP Munich, Court Orchestra under Strauss, 2 March 1887.

München
1st Version: An occasional waltz for orchestra. 1938–39. Not performed. Manuscript.
2nd Version: A Memorial Waltz for orchestra. 1945. No opus number. WP Vienna, Symphony Orchestra under Fritz Lehmann, 21 March 1951.

Japanische Festmusik
For the 2600th anniversary of the Japanese Empire. 1940. Opus 84. WP Tokyo, Japan; United Symphony Orchestra under H. Fellmer, 11 December 1940.

Metamorphosen
Study for 23 solo strings in C minor. 1944–45. No opus number. WP Zürich, Collegium Musicum under Paul Sacher, 25 January 1946.

CHAMBER MUSIC

String Quartet in A
1879–80. Opus 2. WP Munich, Walter Quartet

Cello Sonata in F
1881–83. Opus 6. WP Nuremberg, Hans Wihan and Hildegard von Königsthal, 8 December 1883.

Piano Quartet in C minor
1883–84. Opus 13. WP Weimar, Halir Quartet and Strauss (piano). 8 December 1885.

Violin Sonata in E♭
1887–88. Opus 18. WP Elberfeld, Robert Heckmann and Julius Buths, 3 October 1888.

The following works, although generally performed under a conductor, are more properly designated as chamber music, and are therefore shown here:

Serenade for 13 Wind Instruments in E♭
1881–82. Opus 7. WP Dresden Tonkunstlerverein Wind instruments under Franz Wüllner, 27 November 1882.

Suite for 13 Wind Instruments in B♭
1883–84. Opus 4. WP Munich, Wind of Meiningen Court Orchestra under Strauss, 18 November 1884.

1st Sonatina for 16 Wind Instruments in F
1943. No opus number. 'From the workshop of an invalid'. WP Dresden, Wind of the State Orchestra under Karl Elmendorff, 18 June 1944.

2nd Sonatina for 16 Wind Instruments in E♭
1944–45. No opus number. 'From the Merry Workshop'.
WP Winterthur, Musikkollegium, Stadtorchester under Hermann Scherchen, 25 March 1946.

PIANO MUSIC

Five Piano Pieces 1880–81. Opus 3.
Piano Sonata in B minor 1880–81. Opus 5.
Five Voice-pictures for Piano 1883–84. Opus 9.
Improvisations and Fugue on an original theme 1884. No opus number. Manuscript.

RECITATIONS FOR VOICE AND PIANO

Enoch Arden (Tennyson)
A melodrama after the translation by A. Strodtmann. 1897. Opus 38. WP Munich, February 1897, Ernst von Possart and Strauss.
Das Schloss am Meer (Uhland).
A melodrama. 1899. No opus number. WP Berlin, 23 March 1899, Ernst von Possart and Strauss.

WORKS FOR OTHER KEYBOARD INSTRUMENTS

Hochzeitspräludium for 2 harmoniums.
Composed for the wedding of Dr. Franz Strauss and Alice Grab. 1924. No opus number. Vienna 15 January 1924: played by Strauss and Karl Alwin.
Capriccio Suite for harpsichord.
1944. (Opus 85). Manuscript. WP Vienna Konzerthaus (Mozart-Saal) 7 November 1946 by Isolde Ahlgrimm.

SONGS FOR VOICE AND PIANO (Subsequent orchestrations noted)

Eight Songs from 'Letzte Blätter' by Hermann von Gilm. 1882–83. Opus 10. No. 1 orchestrated by Strauss; Nos. 1 and 8 orchestrated by Robert Heger. (*Zueignung* and *Allerseelen*)
Three Love Songs (Stieler, Sallet, Gruppe). 1883–84. No opus number.
Five Songs (Michelangelo, von Schack). 1884–86. Opus 15. No.57 (*Heimkehr*) orchestrated by L. Weniger.
Six Songs after poems by F. von Schack. 1887. Opus 17. No.2 (*Ständchen*) orchestrated by Felix Mottl.
Schlichte Weisen. Five poems by Felix Dahn. 1887–88. Opus 21.
Two Songs after poems by Nicklaus Lenau. 1891–93. Opus 26.
Four Songs (Henckell, Hart, Mackay). 1893–94. Opus 27.
No. 1 *Ruhe Meine Seele*, No. 2 *Cäcilie* and No. 4 *Morgen!* orchestrated by Strauss; No. 3 *Heimliche Aufforderung* orchestrated by Heger.
Three Songs after poems by Otto J. Bierbaum. 1894–95. Opus 29.
No. 1 *Traum durch die Dämmerung* orchestrated by Heger.
Four Songs (Busse, Dehmel). 1896. Opus 31.
Wir beide wollen springen (Bierbaum). 1896. No opus number.
Five Songs (Henckell, Liliencron, *Wunderhorn*). 1896. Opus 32
No. 1 *Ich trage meine Minne* orchestrated by Heger; No. 3 *Liebeshymnus* by Strauss.
Four Songs (Klopstock, *Wunderhorn*, Rückert). 1898. Opus 36.
No. 1 *Das Rosenband* orchestrated by Strauss.
Six Songs (Liliencron, Falke, Dehmel, Bodman, Lindner). 1897–98. Opus 37. No. 2 *Ich liebe dich*, No. 3 *Meinem Kinde* and No. 4. *Mein Auge* orchestrated by Strauss.
Five Songs (Dehmel, Bierbaum). 1897–98. Opus 39. No. 3. *Der Arbeitsmann* and No. 4 *Befreit* orchestrated by Strauss.
Five Songs (Dehmel, Mackay, Liliencron, Morgenstern). 1899. Opus 41. No. 1 *Wiegenlied* orchestrated by Strauss.
Three Songs after classical German Poets. (Klopstock, Bürger, Uhland). 1899. Opus 43. No. 2 *Muttertändelei* orchestrated by Strauss.
Five Songs after poems by Friedrich Rückert. 1899–1900. Opus 46.
Five Songs after poems by Ludwig Uhland. 1900. Opus 47.
No. 2 *Des Dichters Abendgang* orchestrated by Strauss.
Five Songs (Bierbaum, Henckell). 1900. Opus 48. No. 1 *Freundliche Vision*, No. 4 *Winterweihe*, No. 5 *Winterliebe* all orchestrated by Strauss
Eight Songs (Dehmel, Henckell, Panizza, *Wunderhorn*,). 1900–01. Opus 49. No. 1 *Waldseligkeit* orchestrated by Strauss.
Two Songs from Calderón's play *Richter von Zalamea* for guitar or harp accompaniment. 1904. No opus number.
Six Songs (Goethe, Henckell, C. F. Meyer, Heine). 1903–06.

Opus 56. No. 1 *Frühlingsfeier* orchestrated by Strauss. No. 6 *Die heiligen drei Könige* can only be properly performed in its orchestrated version by Strauss.
Krämerspiegel. Twelve Songs after poems by Alfred Kerr. 1918. Opus 66.
Six Songs (Shakespeare, Goethe). 1918. Opus 67.
Six Songs after poems by Clemens von Brentano. 1918. Opus 68.
Five Little Songs (von Arnim, Heine). 1918. Opus 69.
Five Oriental Songs to poems by Hans Bethge after excerpts from the 'Hafiz' and 'Chinese Flute'. 1928. Opus 77.
Four Songs for bass. (Rückert, Goethe). 1922–35. Opus '87'.
Three Songs (Anon., Weinheber). 1933–42. Opus '88'. No. 1 *Das Bächlein* orchestrated by Strauss.
Xenion (Goethe). 1942. No opus number.

SONGS WITH ORCHESTRA

Four Songs (Mackay, von Bodman, Anon., Goethe). 1896–97. Opus 33. 3 December 1900.
Two large-scale songs for low voice (Dehmel, Rückert). 1899. Opus 44. WP Berlin Philharmonic. Baptist Hoffmann. Strauss.
Two songs for deep bass (Uhland, Heine). 1902–06. Opus 51.
Three Hymns after poems by Hölderin. 1921. WP Berlin Volksoper Barbara Kemp, G. Brecher, 9 November, 1921.
Four Songs (Eichendorff, Hesse). 1948. No opus number. The 'Four Last Songs'. WP London, Albert Hall. Kirsten Flagstad and Philharmonia Orchestra under Wilhelm Furtwängler 22 May 1950.

CHORAL WORKS

1) *Unaccompanied*
Schwäbische Erbschaft (F. Loewe) for 4-part male chorus. 1885. No opus number. WP Mönchen-Gladbach, 7 October 1950.
Schzerquartett 'Utan svafvel och Fosfor'. Male voices. 1889. No opus number. WP Weimar 14 December 1890, Hofkapelle under Strauss.
Two Male-Voice Choruses from Herder's *Stimmen der Völker*. 1899. Opus 42. WP Vienna Schubertbund, 8 December 1899.
Three Male-Voice Choruses from Herder's *Stimmen der Völker*. 1899. Opus 45.
Six Folksong Arrangements
1906 Berlin, 6 March 1907 under Strauss.
Deutsche Motette for 4 solo voices and 16-part mixed chorus, after words by Friedrich Rückert. 1913. Opus 62. WP Berlin, Hofmannsthal, theatre Singchor under H. Rüdel, 2 December 1913.
Cantata for male chorus by Hugo von Hofmannsthal. 1914. No opus number.
Three Male-Voice Choruses after poems by Rückert. 1935. No opus number. Cologne, Male Voice Chorus under Papst, 29 March, 1936.
Die Göttin im Putzzimmer (Rückert) for 8-part mixed chorus. 1935. WP Vienna State Opera Chorus under Krauss, 2 March, 1952.
Durch Einsamkeiten (Wildgans) for male chorus. 1939. No opus number. Vienna Schubertbund under Nurrer, 1 April 1939.

2) *Orchestrally accompanied*
Wandrers Sturmlied (Goethe) for 6-part chorus and full orchestra. 1884. Opus 14. WP Cologne, City Orchestra and Chorus under Strauss, 8 March 1887.
Bardengesang (Klopstock) for male chorus and orchestra. 1886. No opus number. WP Meiningen Court Theatre under Strauss, February 1886 (Manuscript lost).
Hymne for female chorus and orchestra, with wind band. 1897. No opus number. WP Munich, Court Orchestra and Chorus under Strauss, 1 June, 1897.
Taillefer
Ballad by Uhland for Soli, Chorus and Orchestra. 1902–03. Opus 52. WP Heidelberg Music Festival Orchestra under Strauss, 26 October, 1903.
Bardengesang (2nd Version) for 3 male-voice choruses and orchestra. 1906. Opus 55. WP Dresden Teachers' Choral Society and Gewerbehauskapelle under F. Brandes, 6 February 1907.

Die Tageszeiten
Song Cycle after poems by Eichendorff for male chorus and orchestra. 1928. Opus 76. Vienna, Schubert Bund under Viktor Keldorfer, 21 July, 1928.

Austria
Austrian Song by A. Wildgans for full orchestra and male chorus. 1929. Opus 78. WP Vienna Männergesangverein under F. Grossmann, 20 January 1930

Olympische Hymne (R. Lubahn) for mixed chorus and full orchestra. 1936. No opus number. For the opening of the 1936 Berlin Olympiad on 1 August 1936: masses choirs under Strauss.

An den Baum Daphne
Epilogue to the opera *Daphne* for 9-part mixed chorus. 1943. No opus number. Vienna State Opera Chorus and Boys' Choir under Felix Prohaska, 5 January, 1947.

Further Reading List

Baum, Günther *Richard Strauss und Hugo von Hofmannsthal* (Berlin, 1962)
Bie, Oscar *Moderne Musik und Richard Strauss* (Berlin, 1916)
Böhm, Karl *Begegnung mit Richard Strauss* (Vienna-Munich, 1964)
Del Mar, Norman *Richard Strauss* Vols. I, II, III (London 1962, 1969, 1972)
Geissmar, Berta *The Baton and the Jackboot* (London, 1944)
Gregor, Joseph *Richard Strauss, der Meister der Oper* (Munich, 1939)
Hammelmann, Hanns *Hofmannsthal* (London, 1957)
Jefferson, Alan *The Operas of Richard Strauss in Britain 1910–1963* (London, 1963)
—*The Lieder of Strauss* (London, 1971)
—*Richard Strauss* (Newton Abbot, 1973)
Krause, Ernst *Richard Strauss. The Man and his Work* (London, 1964)
Mann, William *The Operas of Richard Strauss* (London, 1964)
Marek, George *Richard Strauss: The Life of a non-Hero* (London, 1967)
Myers, Rollo (ed.) *Richard Strauss: Romain Rolland. Correspondence Diary and Essays* (London, 1968)
Newman, Ernest *Richard Strauss* (London, 1921)
Pander, Oscar von *Clemens Krauss* (Munich, 1955)
Panofsky, Walter *Richard Strauss: Partitur eines Lebens* (Munich, 1965)
Russell, John *Erich Kleiber* (London, 1957)
Steinitzer, Max *Richard Strauss.* (4th and 12th Editions) (Berlin, 1911, 1927)
—*Richard Strauss in seiner Zeit* (Leipzig, 1914)
STRAUSS, Richard *Recollections and Reflections* (London, 1949)
—*Correspondence with Hofmannsthal* (London, 1961)
Tenschert, Roland *3×7 Variationen über das Thema Richard Strauss* (Vienna, 1944)
Trenner, Franz *Dokumente seines Lebens und Schaffens* (Munich, 1954)
Schuh, Willi (ed.) Richard Strauss Yearbook 1954 (Bonn, 1953) 1959/60 (Bonn, 1960)
Trenner, Franz and Schuh, Willie (ed.) *Correspondence between Richard Strauss and Hans von Bülow* (London, 1953)
Wagner, Friedelind The Royal Family of Bayreuth (London, 1948)

Index

Picture Acknowledgements

The publishers would like to thank the following for permission to reproduce their material:

Alan Jefferson: 14, 15b, 74r
Albertina, Vienna: 26/27
Bob Anderson: 56t, 56b
Bayerische Staatsbibliothek: 85
Harry R. Beard Theatre Collection: 61br, 70
Boosey and Hawkes: 8c, 8br, 10t
Gunn Brinson: 95
C.B.S. Records Ltd: 38b
William Gordon Davis: 61tr
Houston Rogers: 81l, 81b
Archiv für Kunst und Geschichte: 11, 12, 13, 15r, 37, 38, 41t, 46, 59, 60, 61bl, 64, 73, 74, 107
Mansell Collection: 21, 24t, 28, 53, 103
Metropolitan Opera Guild, New York: 68
André Meyer: 63
Österreichische Nationalbibliothek: 6, 8tr, 9, 19, 20, 32, 33, 44, 58b, 81t, 82b, 83, 86, 94, 98/99b
Robert Ponsonby: 23
Archiv der Pschorr A.G., Munich: 8tl
Dr Kate Roth: 41b
Richard Strauss Gesellschaft: 49, 98l
Süddeutscher Verlag: 50, 88, 89, 90, 92, 97
Professor Hans Swarosky: 72
Ullstein Bilderdienst: 35, 39, 40, 43, 45t, 75, 104, 106
Reg Wilson: 55, 65, 66/67, 77
Roger Wood: 62bl, 62tl, 62t
Zentralbibliothek der deutschen Klassik, Weimar: 57